INSIDE JAPAN:

ITS PEOPLE AND CULTURE

Felipe CoFreros, Ph.D.

Order this book online at www.trafford.com
or email orders@trafford.com

Most Trafford titles are also available at major online book retailers.

Senior Editors:	Ronald Jay Blassingame, Ph.D.
	Janet Villagomez, Ph.D.
Associate Editors:	Yolanda Delariarte De Stefano, Ed. D.
	Cindy Jordan, R.N.
	Charlene Rose Escolango CoFreros
Title Design:	Chaplain Romeo Tomas Salovino BCC
	Engineer Filomeno "Jun" Faldas Jr.
	Cornelius H. CoFreros

Print information available on the last page.

ISBN: 978-1-4907-8920-0 (sc)
ISBN: 978-1-4907-8921-7 (e)

Trafford rev. 06/04/2018

www.trafford.com
North America & international
toll-free: 1 888 232 4444 (USA & Canada)
fax: 812 355 4082

CONTENTS

PREFACE

This book "Inside Japan: Its People and Culture" is designed for those who are eager to acquaint themselves with Japan, its culture, people, and innovative technology.

The contents of this book have been prompted by the necessity to expose the readers to "Inside Japan: Its People and Culture." Much of what has been chosen here represents Japan in the 21st century. This book may afford the readers the exposure of Japan and the awareness of the Japanese people not only to its neighbors in the North Pacific Region but to the rest of the world.

For foreign nationals who have an urgent need to acquire knowledge of what's the role of Japan in the international community, this book offers a ready reference and a practical approach. This book has been developed and is dedicated to the great people of Japan, for their example, friendship, and devotion to all things worth.

The materials have been called from the author's many years of experience as a columnist and editor-in-chief of the Philippines English Newspaper based in Nagoya City, Japan. The articles are enriched by pertinent examples taken mostly from actual research by the author in the Land of the Rising Sun, Japan.

It is aspired that this book "Inside Japan: Its People and Culture" will be more responsive to the reader's need and interest and at the same time give insights to people who wants to understand Japanese as they are.

Felipe CoFreros Ph.D.

INTRODUCTION

This book "Inside Japan: Its People and Culture" tackles Japan's position in the 21ˢᵗ century. It tells Japans' role in the international community to maintain its current position in the future by making its views be understood by foreign nationals.

Although, Japanese people are in-conspicuous to make their way of thinking and behavior fully understood by foreign nationals due to their traditional beliefs, they find ways to engage themselves with the international community, for if they continue to stay mum politically, while keeping their economic might, it will be difficult for them to maintain their international standing they are enjoying.

In addition, the nation's political, economic and social system revamped simultaneously and Japan embarks on such reforms while they can still afford to do so.

Japan also cooperates with the United States of America (USA) being the superpower in ensuring the stability of the new global order in the 21ˢᵗ century. They are also doing this with other Asian nations where unstable factors are huge because of diverse economic and political conditions. Japan does not only provide economic aid to Asian neighbors but also promote friendship and trust through exchanges in various fields.

Felipe CoFreros Ph.D.

ACKNOWLEDGMENTS

I wish to express my deep gratitude and sincere appreciation to the following people who in one way or another assisted me in making this book possible.

To Ronald Jay Blassingame, Ph.D., Janet Villagomez Ph.D., Yolanda Delariarte De Stefano, Ed.D. who greatly rendered their services with the editing; Marlon L. Patalagsa, Candido Magnaye, Imelda Orda Schwartz, Rosemarie Espiritu Parreno, Lolita Gamboa, Sean Gamboa, Marilyn Omalin, Larry Omalin, Victoria Pardo Long, Hope Villanueva Blassingame, John Shafer, Teresita Magbanua-Shafer M.A., Caryl Anne Diamante-Depositario, Leonor Antoja Verano M.A., Nestor Tebio M.A., Matsy Balan-eg Tumaedang, John Duffy, Thomas Rogers, Rolf Klemm, Joeanne Marie Sabido Diamante-Jomalesa M.A., Franz Josef Diamante Valerie Sabido Carillo RN, Hannah Katrina Sabido-Montallana RN, Pamela Anne B. Sabido, Norma Salmo-Ardiente, M.A., Linda Salmo, Cindy Jordan, R.N. Maria Luisa Sabido-Assin, Beltran Assin, Lexie Lou Sabido-Carillo, Donna Sabido Assin-Abayon MBA, Antonio Abayon MBA, Carlo Sabido Assin, Eden Arcellana-Asin, Mary Jane Sabido Alvaran-Ong RN, Jennifer Sabido Alvaran Hofilena RN, Eva Sabido Daliva RN, Edwin Daliva, Maria Luz Sabido-Carillo RN, Engineer Alexander Carillo, Kimberly Daliva-Yaneza, RN, Jesserie Alvaran-Faley, Salvador Sabido Jr., Jenna Balasbas Sabido, Cecilia Sabido Hallares,

Benjamen Hallares, Michael Angelo Sabido, Nanette Sabido Rabino, Jo Ann Sabido-Agreda, Maria Therese Sabido Lim, Anecita Sabido-Diamante, Engineer Jose Diamante, Filomeno "Jun" Faldas Jr., Cristina Manalo-Vaughn, Terrence Vaughn, Virginia Sabido, Raul Arensol Sabido, Cheryl Lynn T. Rojas-Sabido RN, Elma Escolango CoFreros, Caroline Cuarenta CoFreros, Alona Pascual, Ricardo Pascual, Chaplain Romeo Tomas Salovino, BCC who collaborated with me on this book, and to my son Cornelius Hiponia CoFreros and my daughter Charlene Rose Escolango CoFreros and to Mr. Charlie M. Gaddi who glean and offered suggestions on the material.

I received a great deal of encouragement and cooperation from Reverend Masachika Terada and Noriko Kajiwara Director and Assistant Director, Saint Mary College/Nunoike Culture Center 1-12-23, A01, Higashi-ku, Nagoya City, Japan.

To the staff of Chubu Philippines Friendship Association in Japan, Nagoya City Chapter, Ms. Linda Taki, Ms. Helen Noda, Ms. Terry Morooka, Ms. Maria Luisa Fukuzawa, Ms. Cynthia Shinoda, Ms. Myrna Mendoza, Mr. Fumio Naitoh, Ms. Melanie Kojima, Ms. Mellienor Sahara, Ms. Elizabeth Kan, Ms. Lourdes Nepomuceno, Fr. John Seland, SVD, Nanzan University, Nagoya City, Japan, Ms. Belen Yamagata, Atty. Barbara Uchida and Reverend Toru A. Nishimoto, Chaplain of the Japanese National in the Philippines for their enormous support to have this book realized.

To the staff of the Philippines English Newspaper based in Nagoya City, Japan: Mr. Bernabe J. Sanchez, Mr. Nestor A. Mariano, Engineer Jesus G. Abubo, Mr. Marcy G. Carolino, Ms. Margie C. Ieda, Ms. Mercedes A. Ishihara, Ms. Marissa Mercado and Mr. Keiichi Kasuga for their patronage, counsel and recommendations.

To Ms. Maria Stella Arensol Peralta and Ms. Odessa Arensol Peralta who made all efforts for compiling and for the tedious work of typing the manuscript of this book.

Finally, to my Japanese students in Saint Mary College/Nunoike Culture Center, Nagoya City, Japan who shared their insights about Japan, its people, culture and innovative technology which inspired me to go through the process of making this book possible for them.

Felipe CoFreros Ph.D.

ABOUT THE AUTHOR

Felipe Cofreros spent twenty five years of aggregate experience in teaching literacy, adult education, pre-school, elementary, high school, college and the administration of instructional English as a Second language [ESL] services among Indo-Chinese refugees [Vietnamese, Lao, Khmer and Hmong] in the International Catholic Migration Commission [ICMC], Philippine Refugee Processing Center [PRPC] in Sabang, Morong, Bata-an, Philippines for a decade. Felipe also taught English as a Second Language [ESL] in different countries in Asia and North America: Saint Mary College in Nagoya City, Japan for two years;

Regent College and Pannasastra University of Cambodia in Samdech Pann, Phnom Penh, Kingdom of Cambodia for two years; The United Nations [UN] Language Center in Dili City and Manufahi district in East Timor for two years; Zoni Language Centers in Manhattan and Queens, New York City, New York, United States of America [USA] for seven years and Effective Tutoring Systems in Las Vegas, Nevada, United States of America for three years.

Felipe's vast experience as a curriculum developer in Arts and Crafts program in the International Catholic Migration Commission [ICMC], Preparation for the American Secondary School [PASS] Program in the Philippine Refugee Processing Center in Sabang, Morong, Bata-an, Philippines; Saint Mary College in Nagoya City, Japan; University of Saint La Salle in Bacolod City, Philippines; La Consolacion College in Bacolod City, Philippines and Assumption Convent School in Iloilo City, Philippines greatly contributed to the creation of the following books that he wrote: A Handbook of Basic Art, Part 1 [Painting Processes in Playing with Colors, Different Crayon Techniques]; A Handbook of Basic Art, Part II [Basic Drawing, Painting and Making Crafts] and Let's Weave [An Ancient Hand Art of Interlacing Two Groups of Threads]. He has also written more than a dozen of Children's Picture Books with illustrations and comprehension questions: A Pre-school Math Workbook "Let's Build Our Math Skills Workbook" For children ages three years old and up; Inside Japan: Its People and Culture and Effective Ways To Assess English Language Learners [For Intermediate and Advanced Levels].

Felipe graduated as scholar or its equivalent to cum laude from the University of San Agustin in Iloilo City, Philippines with a Bachelor of Science in Elementary Education with specialization in Social Studies and Art Education. He got his Latin, Spanish and Theology courses at the Seminary of San Agustin in Intramuros, Manila, Philippines and a Master of Arts credits in Language and Literature Program, Teaching English as a Second Language [ESL] in De La Salle University in Manila, Philippines.

He got his Master's Degree in TESOL and Doctor of Philosophy in Sociology from an on-line university in the U.S.A.

Felipe obtained quite a number of certificates in different disciplines such as: TESOL Teaching Certificate Course, Lingua Edge, LCC, TESOL Teacher Training Systems at West Olympic Blvd., Beverly Hills, California, USA; Managing People for Maximum Performance in John F. Kennedy School of Management, Harvard University in Cambridge, Massachusetts, USA; The Roots of Learning: Society for Effective Affective Learning in Brighton, England, United Kingdom; Basic Japanese Language and Japanese Sumie Art in Saint Mary College, Nagoya City, Japan and the New Role of Art in Education in the University of the Philippines in Iloilo City, Philippines.

BOOKS BY FELIPE COFREROS PH.D.

Children's Picture Books

The Hungry Frog
Danny The Deer
Blue Bird
Blue Bird Finds New Friends
Blue Bird and The Bees
Blue Bird and Black Bird
The Little Birds Help A Friend
The Boastful Rooster
Smart Ratty
Ollie and His Ball
Ollie Lost His Ball
Fix it Tipsie
Sam's Wish
Curious Sam
Sam and The Little Bird
Sam and The Hawk
Jackie's New Toy

Other Books

A Pre-school Math Workbook: Let's Start Building Our Math Skills Workbook (For Three Years Old and Up)

Inside Japan: Its People and Culture

Effective Ways To Assess English Language Learners (For Intermediate and Advanced Levels)

A Handbook of Basic Art, Part I (Painting Processes in Playing With Colors, Different Crayon Techniques)

A Handbook of Basic Art, Part II (Basic Drawing, Painting and Making Crafts)

Let's Weave (An Ancient Hand Art of Interlacing Two Groups of Thread)

A Handbook of Writing Activities For Intermediate and Advanced English Language Learners

One Accord - An Inspirational book of Bible Promises

WHAT'S INSIDE JAPAN?

The Japanese are, to the highest degree, both aggressive and unaggressive, both militaristic and aesthetic, both insolvent and polite, loyal and treacherous, brave and timid, conservative and hospitable in new ways. The Japanese are human beings just like everyone else, but they have a strong authoritarian tradition. Though now a democracy, past governments have undeniably put restraints on its people's minds so that individuality in Japan is not what it is elsewhere. But even this is fast changing as Japan competes in an open market-place. Internationalism is breaking down these restraints.

Japanese men are without doubt the best disciplined workers in the world. They are concerned about the quality of their products and the image of their company. They work long hours - versus a 35-hour work week in much of the West - do not think of leisure as a right. The average Japanese spends two months more in his office or factory than the average American, and nearly three months most than the average West German. He is demonstrably less individualistic than his Western counterpart because of peer pressure to conform. Thus, drinking, tennis, and golf are his common leisure activities because that is what his peers are doing. Little Japanese boys are so protected by their mothers that they often lack a strong sense of self. Eventually, their company becomes a kind of ersatz mother, at least in the case of a typical salaried man.

Overtime work and ailments due to stress may account in part for Japan's rising divorce rate which has more than doubled over the past 20 years. Lonely wives who become kitchen alcoholics are yet another result of the husband's absence from the home. One Japanese wife sadly wrote to a Tokyo newspaper - "My husband and I are like friendly strangers."

Japanese husbands, on the other hand, are often victims of great stress. It is a superior's responsibility to try and reduce pressures afflicting his men. The worst of it is that these bosses are often themselves victims of stress - a kind of vicious cycle. Then there is the question of promotion. Today, most workers will not, as in the past, advance to a managerial post. Psychologically, this is damaging to the workers' morale. The government is trying to introduce the concept of leisure time into the workplace, but the situation remains unchanged. Japan is crowded and life is highly competitive and expensive.

It is a credit to Japan's medical profession and diet that the Japanese today live longer than most other people. The average Japanese man will live to 75, while the average Japanese women lives to more than 80 years. Is this a good thing for the nation? Perhaps not. In 1950, less than 5 percent of the population was over 65, but by 1986 the figure had risen to 10.3 percent. In another 20 years, it is predicted that Japan will have the world's highest proportion of the elderly. This will affect three main areas: the workplace, the health and welfare of Japanese citizens, and the family. Can Japan absorb all the young workers coming along without laying-off older individuals at, say, 55 years of age? Statistics are mixed. But keeping highly-paid older workers on the payroll is increasingly a problem specially for the small to the middle-size companies. The seniority system, ten, may no longer be fitted for the Japan of tomorrow. Nor retirement bonuses either. Some firms are already replacing such bonuses with pension plans in order to ease the financial burden.

Less critical, perhaps, is the question of looking after the health of the elderly. By the year 2030, it is believed that there will be some 16 million bedridden senior citizens - more than twice the figure today. This will put a great burden on Japan's health care facilities and personnel. It will also cause the country's medical bill to more than triple over the next 15 years. Nursing homes are now in great demand, especially as fewer young Japanese are willing to look after their elderly family members. We must not forget that the elderly do not want to be a burden. At the same time, they deserve humane, loving care. Loneliness is another affliction of the elderly. As Japan's birth-rate continues to fall, this problem is bound to grow more acute. Japanese must prepare for the demands an ageing population will make in the future.

The time to act is now. Japan, as an industrialized country, has dealt with her social problems better than most Western countries. The Japanese are well equipped to meet the challenges that lie ahead.

THE GRAYING SOCIETY IN JAPAN

Some of Japan's largest corporations have introduced a system of personnel management under which middle managers aged 45 or older are given an opportunity to take a break from their daily routines to reorient their careers.

This phenomenon is the result of two factors. The first is that the Japanese companies have been forced to re-examine the personnel practices they had regarded as gospel during the years of uninterrupted economic growth: lifetime employment, seniority-based wages, and the system of mandatory retirement.

The second is that Japanese people are living longer. In 1955 the average life expectancy of Japanese males was 63.6 years. Today, they can expect to live to nearly 80. If those who retire at 60 live on to 80, they will have 20 years with nothing to do. Those who retire when they are only 50 will have to spend 30 years doing nothing.

Given the longer life spans of the Japanese there is a need to rethink the age at which we part with our jobs, and we also need to think about how we spend our post-retirement years. We must keep in mind, of course, that there are personal differences in both physical strength and ability.

Physical deterioration is unavoidable as we age, but the same cannot be said of our abilities. Personal differences in the capacity to perform productively probably widen as we advance in age.

For instance, I learned that a 75-year-old woman had enrolled in my English Language class for Japanese professionals. I looked over the some 30 students in the room, but to my surprise I was unable to find her.

At the next class I looked around again more carefully. This time I was able to locate her, and I realized why I had so much trouble locating her the first time.

I had been looking for an aged, "75-year-old" woman, but the woman who had enrolled in my class did not look a day over 60. She had a cheery expression, a straight back, and wore fashionable and attractive clothes. I asked her why she had enrolled in my English Language class. Her response was clear and to the point: "When I'm with people my own age, the conversation tends to focus on a narrow range of subjects. I want to broaden my horizons and learn new things." Although the woman was my mother's age, I found myself identifying with her strongly.

Several weeks later, I attended a party for Mr. Noda, a good friend of mine, to celebrate his 70th birthday and commemorate his appointment as special adviser in his company. In his address to assembled guests, he claimed that the real work was still ahead of him. "I want to do all I can to make Japan a better society on behalf of all my wartime friends who died during World War II," he said, "I'm particularly concerned about the war orphans left behind in China and want to devote my remaining years to securing their happiness." His speech was greeted with enthusiastic applause.

Both the 75-year-old woman in my English Language class and the 70-year-old Mr. Noda are active members of the graying society in Japan. As this thought crossed my mind, I realized that there are many more such Japanese people around me.

For instance, the honorary Director of Saint Mary College in Nagoya, Japan, the Reverend Masachika Terada is past 70. His address at a graduation ceremony for the school was full of youthful vigor and brought the house down. He talked engagingly about his job and urged listeners to lead fuller lives. "There's no time like this very moment to get started on the life you really aspire to," he said.

Reaching a conclusion on how long we should continue working becomes difficult in the light of such examples. We cannot assume that people's productivity will begin deteriorating at around age 50 or 60 as our bodies grow more frail. There are plenty of people who are 70 or older who can outperform those in their 30s and 40s.

There are serious drawbacks to compelling people to quit when they reach a certain age through legal constraints and corporate rules. An ideal system is one based on merit rather than age, one that will force even those in their 30s to quit if they are not making a contribution to the company and will keep on the payroll those in their 70s who are mentally sharp and are performing a valuable function in the company.

The Japanese are now entering an age when each company needs to measure the ability of its employees more precisely and systematically and to introduce a more flexible system of mandatory retirement.

THE UPS AND DOWNS OF AGING IN JAPAN

A good many years ago, I traveled in the mountains of Mount Kanlaon in central Philippines together with my grade seven students from the De La Salle University in Bacolod City, Negros Occidental, Philippines to visit people of a certain ethnic minority group. At one point in the journey, I had to descent a terraced rock formation that dropped about 500 meters like a natural staircase.

At first, the going was easy, and I was humming to myself. But I hadn't gone one-third of the way when my knees and back began to feel the strain. Pain intensified with each step and by the time I reach my place of lodging, I was practically crawling on floors. Descending is much more extraneous than ascending. You can over-strain and hurt your legs.

I thought about these ABCs of hiking as I lay sprawled on the bed receiving an emergency treatment from a local acupuncturist. Now that I suffer from mild but chronic neuralgia, I can say with full conviction that you don't have to be descending a mountain to experience such discomfort.

Climbing the stairs is not too bad. But when going down, I should really watch my step. I could pay dearly for carelessly descending a long staircase at a subway station in Tokyo, Japan, for instance.

For this reason, I could not agree more with what authoritic Ms. H. Noda pointed out in her column in one popular Health magazine for women in Japan.

Just two decades ago, an overwhelming majority of escalators at train stations in Tokyo go up only, Ms. H. Noda observed, eventhough descending the stairs is much more dangerous and time-consuming for people with disabilities.

Ideally, she argued every train station should have two escalators - one going up and another going down. But if this is not feasible, the single escalator should be for descent.

Installing only an Up escalator is "Kind and Considerate" only to people who have no disabilities.

Japan is an aging society, there will soon be a rapid increase in the number of people reaching old age including the multiethnic society, and they will be feeling it unmistakably in the loss of youthful spring from gait. These people may be able to get around on their feet without too much problem, but descending a staircase is a different matter altogether.

In calling for Down escalators at train stations, Ms. H. Noda continued, "I have been reiterating my argument whenever possible, but I see no signs of change. I believe this is because the absence of change is not going to cause any business to go belly up.....

'Even in this age of competition, technology and liberalization as we are in the early part of the 21st century, the prevailing attitude of the train industry in Japan is to let users keep coming back if they want, really serving and treating them with an average comfort of travelling in a couch with iron wheels.

THE VALUE OF TIME IN JAPAN

For Japanese, time is a resource that, like water or coal, can be use well or poorly. "Time is money," they say. "You only get so much time in this life; you'd best use it wisely. "The future will not be better than the past or the present, as Japanese are trained to see things, unless people use their time for constructive, future-oriented activities. Thus, Japanese admire a well organized person, one who has a written list of things to do and a schedule for doing them. The ideal person is punctual (that is, arrives at the scheduled time for a meeting or event) and is considerate of other people's time (that is, does not waste people's time with conversation or other activity that has no visible, beneficial outcome).

The Japanese attitude toward time is not necessarily shared by others, especially non-Europeans. They are more likely to conceive time as something that is simply there around them, not something they can use. One of the more difficult things many foreign businessmen and students must adjust to in Japan is the notion that time must be saved whenever possible and used wisely everyday.

In their efforts to use their time wisely, Japanese are sometimes seen by foreign visitors as automators, inhuman creatures who are so tied to their clocks and schedules that they cannot participate in or enjoy the human interactions that are truly important things in life. "They are like little machines running around," one foreign visitor said.

The premium Japanese place on efficiency is closely related to their concepts of the future, change and time. To do something efficiently is to do it in a way that is quickest and requires the smallest expenditure of resources. Japanese businesses sometimes hire "efficiency experts" to review their operation and suggest ways in which they could accomplish more than they are currently accomplishing with the resources they are investing. Popular periodicals carry suggestions for more efficient ways to shop, cook, clean house, do errands, raise children, tend the yard and on and on.

In this context the (Obento-food industry can be seen as a clear example of the Japanese cultural product. The Obento and other fast food establishments prosper in a country where many people want to minimize the amount of time they spend preparing and eating meals. The millions of Japanese who take their meals at Obento - food restaurants cannot have much interest in lingering over food while conversing with friends, as millions as Europeans do. As "Obento" and other fast-food restaurants spread around Japan, they have been viewed as symbols of Japanese society and culture, bringing not just Su-shi but an emphasis on speed, efficiency and shiny cleanliness. The typical Japanese food, some observers argue, is Obento, well-prepared, ready to eat food in boxes.

A PERSPECTIVE ABOUT JAPANESE ACTION, WORK AND MATERIALISM

"He's a hard worker," one Japanese might say in praise of another. Or, "She gets the job done." These expressions convey the typical Japanese admiration for a person who approaches a task conscientiously and persistently, seeing it through to a successful conclusion. More than that, these expressions relate an admiration for achievers, people whose lives are centered around efforts to accomplish some physical, measurable thing. Social psychologists use the term "achievement motivation" to describe what appears to be the intention underlying Japanese behaviour. "Affiliation" is another kind of motivation, shown by people whose main intent seems to be establish and retain a set of relationship with other people the achievement motivation predominates in Japan.

Foreign visitors commonly remark that "Japanese work harder than I expected them to." In some "work ethic" may have lost some of its hold on the Japanese, there is still a strong belief that the ideal person is a "hard worker." A hard worker is one who "gets right to work" on a task without delay, work efficiently, completes the task in a way that meets reasonably high standard of a quality. Hard workers are admired not just on the job, but in other aspects of life as well. Housewives, students, and people volunteering their services to charitable organizations can also be "hard workers" who make "significant achievers".

More generally like action. They do indeed believe it is important to devote significant energy to their jobs or other daily responsibilities. Beyond that, they tend to believe they should be doing something most of the time. They are usually not content, as people from other countries are, to sit for hours and talk with other people, they get restless and impatient. They believe they should be doing something, or at best making plans and arrangements for doing something later.

People without the Japanese action orientation often see Japanese as frenzied, always "on the go," never satisfied, compulsively active. They may, beyond that evaluate Japanese negatively for being unable to relax and enjoy life's pleasures. Even recreation, for Japanese, is often a matter of acquiring lavish equipment, making elaborate plans, then going somewhere to do something.

Japanese tend to define people by the job they have. ("Who is he? "He's the vice president in charge of personal loans at the bank.") Their family backgrounds, educational attainments, and other characteristics are considered less important in identifying people than the jobs they have.

There is usually a close relationship between the job a person has and level of the person's income. Japanese tend to measure a person's success in life by referring to the amount of money he has acquired. Being a bank vice president is quite respectable, but being a bank president is more so. The president gets a higher salary. So the president can buy more things - a bigger house and car, more neckties and shoes, and so on.

Japanese are often criticized for being so "materialistic" so concerned with acquiring possessions. For Japanese though, this materialism is natural and power. They have been taught that it is a good thing to achieve - to work hard, acquire more material badges of their success, and in the process assure a better future for themselves and their immediate families. And, like people from elsewhere, they do what they are taught.

THE DIFFERENT VALUES OF
YOUNG JAPANESE

The shadow of decadence is falling over Japan's younger generation. The sense of what is considered to be beautiful and ugly is becoming confused and morals and ethics are degenerating - phenomena which are apt to occur when a culture matures, esp. at the end of the century.

Young people of Japan are exploding established values. Beauty is not always apparent to them, and what others considered to be grotesque proves to be popular. This can be seen in the recent pet trend. For example, many young Japanese women now have lizards or snakes. They are slightly strange. The stranger the better appears to be the belief of modern young people. In the 1990's when fuzzy was the most talked-about word, the standard of values in the Japanese society has been dropping.

Today's youth are characterized by two traits: egotism and the desire to be different. The director of the Japan Youth Research Institute in Sendagaya, Tokyo, said "The young Japanese hate to be dealt with as a group, but they're not individualists either. Doing what they want is their highest priority. This was a typical characteristic of "hitorik-ko (children without any sisters and brothers) and it is now common among all the young Japanese. The now generation of Japanese don't know how to share something with other people. They try to maintain their egotistic attitude toward each other, and they never had a normal relationship.

The young Japanese try to protect their own little world and to keep their circle of friends as small as possible. They're known as "otakkie" a word derived from "otaku" (home), which describes those who prefer to shut themselves into their room instead of going out with friends.

The same thing can be said in young businessmen. "Give and take" is a rule of society, but these people are not in the habit of "giving". They work only for themselves not for their companies, and just "take and take".

The other trait seen in young Japanese is their need to be different. They pay a lot of attention to the differences between themselves, and those who have different lifestyle, and they do everything they can to experience to experience these distinctions. The disparity makes them feel good. "Their desire cannot be classified by psychological methods. According to Abraham Harold Maslow, an American psychologist, a desire will disappear when it has been fulfilled". But the desires of today's young Japanese can never be satisfied. They keep on finding other objects to satisfy their desires to be different. They have the same tendency in their attitude toward love. For example, a woman might have a boyfriend. Even if he loves her very much, she won't be satisfied with only him. She wants to be loved by lots of men at the same time and needs many different kinds of love.

Levi's 501 jeans were the big hit with Japanese teenagers. Used American jeans from the 1960's sold well and sometimes cost more at the second-hand clothes stores in Tokyo. Navy blue blazers with gold buttons, button down shirts and Madras or tartan check patterns were also hits, according to a report titled Hit Products in Japan published by Dentsu Incorporated. Basic items like these became popular with the young Japanese who were attracted by the simple way in which they could dress.

THE WORKING HOURS IN JAPAN

A major challenge for Japanese companies today is to reduce working hours. This is obvious from an international comparison. The average numbers of hours worked annually in 1989 was 2,159 in Japan, compared with 1,957 in the United States, 1,989 in Britain and 1,638 in former West Germany.

The revised Labour Standards Law went into effect in Japan in 1988 to reduce the legal workweek from 48 hours to 40 hours in stages. As a result, the number of regular working hours began to drop. This trend is confirmed by statistics. The figure decreased 1.5-percent in fiscal 1988, 1.2 percent in fiscal in 1989 and 1.2 percent in fiscal in 1990. In fiscal 1991, working hours are estimated to have dropped another 1.5 percent.

Overtime work, however, remains a permanent fixture in the Japanese labour scene. Records show that until recently most workers put in about 14-15 hours of overtime a month. Now that the economy is slowing further, the average number of per capita working hours is likely to drop about 2.1 percent, in part because of reductions in the number of regular working hours. All the same time, the number of regular working hours is likely to decline about 10 percent in fiscal 1991. But overtime work is not likely to disappear.

No less important is the fact that the number of workers has continued to rise despite the economic showdown. When the economy was growing, employers naturally hired more workers. Employment increased 1.3 percent in fiscal 1987, 1.7 percent in fiscal 1988, 2.1 percent in fiscal 1989 and 1.9 percent in fiscal 1990. In fiscal 1991, payrolls are likely to have increased about 1.8 percent. The economy is poised for a further slowdown in the first six months of this year, but the number of workers is still rising at an annual rate of less than 2 percent.

Under these circumstances, businesses are trying hard to reduce their working hours. The demand for labour is diminishing, yet business establishments nation-wide apparently believe now is the best time to hire more workers. That is why employment is continuing to expand despite the slowing of the economy.

The fact is, the Japanese economy is in a "growth recession," meaning that the rate of growth of the gross national product has dropped markedly. The economy is not in the true recession, which is understood to mean two consecutive quarters of declining GNP.

For companies plagued by a profit squeeze, however, the growth recession not be much different from a real recession. For individual workers, it means only a marginal drop in the overtime average of two hours a month.

Japanese wages are not necessarily high by international standards. Consider these statistics. In the case of manufacturing workers, hourly wages for 1989 were ¥ 1,478 in Japan, compared with $11.52 in United States and DM25.77 in the former west Germany. At the yen's average exchange rates against the dollar and the deutsche mark for that year, the American wages were equivalent to ¥ 1,589 and the German wages to ¥ 1,810.

So the problem for Japan, when compared with other industrialized countries, is not that wages are too high, but the working hours are too long for the wages paid. This means that Japanese employers must not only raise wages further but also reduce working hours. On this score, there already exists a broad consensus in both labour and business circles.

Beyond that consensus lies another major issue: labour's share of total business income. This was about 78 percent in 1982 and 1983, for example, but it was nearly 2 percent lower in the late 1980s. What is one to make of this?

One answer is that wage levels are set lower than they should be - in other words, workers are being forced to sacrifice their leisure - by taking less pay than they deserve. Those who hold this view think, and with good reason, that Japan will be treated as the odd man out in the international community unless it changes its ways.

But there is also another, different answer to the question. It is that in the late 1980s employers' share of business income relative to labour's share increased because of inflated asset prices. In this view, labour's share is bound to increase again now that the "bubble economy" has collapsed. There is also much justification for this line of thinking.

Labour's share, of course, varies from country to country depending on the ratio of capital accumulation, such as the ratio of private-sector capital spending to GNP. So it is largely meaningless to make an international comparison of labour's share - meaningless because it does not follow that a higher share in one country is always good and a lower share in another always bad. Countries in the former Soviet bloc, for instance, pursued the goal of expanding labour's share in a given direction on a long-term basis.

The important thing here is to make sure that workers are given more leisure on a longer time basis so that they can enjoy a better life. An international comparison of wage levels, such as given in this article, suggests that the Japanese wage level will go up much further. The problem is that the money made by workers does not have as much purchasing power in Japan as it should.

In 1989, for instance, the yen's purchasing power parity was ¥ 204, much lower than the exchange rate of ¥ 138 to the U.S. dollar, according to a study by the Organization for Economic Cooperation and Development (OECD). This means that Japanese workers were not, and still are not, enjoying their lives in ways commensurate with their wages. That is part of the reason why unions are demanding still higher wage increases.

Even some big-business employers are now saying publicly that wages should be further increased. Such comments are motivated by a realization that Japanese businesses should try to cope in their own ways with the so-called "revisionist thinking" on Japan that has gained currency among foreigners, particularly Americans, in recent years. The revisionists believe that Japan has economic and social structures that are fundamentally different from those of Western countries, and that they should therefore be treated in a different way.

However, a higher wage level is not the right approach to the problem assigned to us. In my view, the best way is to increase the domestic purchasing power of the yen. This can be done, for instance, by bringing down the high prices of agricultural products and services as compared with international norms.

To this end, the domestic market must be opened wider to foreign goods and services, and foreign firms must be given greater freedom to do business in this country. This means, among other things, that Japan needs to change the systems and practices that keep prices high by international standards. In short, what the country needs most is internal reform designed to enable its workers to enjoy a higher standard of living.

MODERN JAPANESE CHOOSE
DIFFERENT LIFESTYLES

All happy families are alike but an unhappy family is unhappy after its own fashion - so **Leo Tolstoy** began **"Anna Karenina."**

This description, however, does not apply to modern Japanese society. It appears that today's Japanese families, whether happy or unhappy, are "after their own fashion."

A young working couple might live apart as they pursue their working careers in different parts of Japan, or even on other sides of the world, and leave their children in the hands of grandparents.

On the other hand, what might appear to be an ordinary happy married couple may not be legally married after all because the woman has decided to keep her maiden name after tying the knot. A married couple, according to Japanese Law, must use the same family name.

While the number of one-member households is increasing, four generation families are emerging in Japan's super-aging society. There are no clear-cut definitions of a family today. Explaining the diversified family styles, today's Japanese family is "consumption-oriented" in contrast with the "production-oriented" family of the past.

"In the old days, family members had to stay together in order to produce food and the other necessities of life, whereas today's family concentrates on spending what they have earned." "Now people are free to choose the family form which most suits them."

"Japan is entering the post nuclear family age where a family is a loosely knit union of people who pursue and lead individual lives," according to Mariko Sugahara, the deputy director general of the National Archive, in "Shin Kazoku no Jidai" (New Family Age).

The conventional concept of a family - a working father, a mother who stays at home and takes care of children - is fading out now that fifty-five percent of married women are working.

Some critics are alarmed. They are afraid that increasing individualism and indifference within a family will eventually lead to the collapse of family life.

In fact, in many Japanese families, members hardly talk to each other and they rarely have dinner together. A father does not come home until midnight. A mother, even a full-time housewife, is not necessarily at home to greet her children when they return from school because she might be attending a flower arrangement class or enjoying another hobby. It is unlikely, any way, that children come home straight from school as more often than not they have to sit through another couple of hours of lectures at a cram school.

One Japanese psychologist calls this type of family a "hotel family," as family members simply share a roof. In a typical hotel family, a living room becomes a dead space, according to architect Mayumi Miyawaki. "The idea of a living room was imported from America after the war as the Japanese family increasingly opted for a nuclear family style. "But a Japanese father comes home only after midnight and a mother packs the children off to study in their own room, so no one uses the living room."

Family gatherings have become such a rare event that a word, "Kazoku susru" (do family), is commonly used to describe the phenomenon. The expression is applicable when family members get together, for example, to have dinner, go to Disneyland or even watch T.V. "The fact that each family member can remain an individual within the family unit is proof of the absence of the oppressive family bond which prevailed in prewar Japan."

Japanese people today draw a positive picture of family life, which is the very reason why they talk about Kazoku suru. Japanese would not think about doing something as a family if they felt heavy family responsibilities. While individualism within a family is becoming a fact of life, more and more Japanese people are now living alone, especially in urban areas. This lifestyle is spreading, not only among the young Japanese, but also among the elderly population, predicting an increased demand from single people or housing.

A good number of elderly people prefer to live alone rather than to inflict themselves on their children. Even if this means living in a tiny shabby apartment room and eating a cup noodle everyday, the elderly people think it is better than being a burden to a young couple. Re-emerging large families are a temporary symptom under the state of emergency or, more exactly, exorbitant land costs and housing expenses. Unlike traditional large Japanese families which were based on the idea of labor sharing, the large families of today are based on nothing but economic convenience. This kind of relationship will not last very long. Meanwhile, the number of young singles is on the rise, due to the increasingly late age at which people are getting married.

A single woman over 25 years of age was once called a Christmas cake, meaning a cake that was past its sale by date of December 25, and of little value. Today the expression is going out of fashion as more and more women find that staying single over the age of 30 is no big deal. Instead, people talk more about the difficulties men face in finding a bride. There is a big gap between a man's concept of an ideal marriage and what women believe. Despite the fact that more and more Japanese women have now become independent financially, Japanese men have been unable to grow out of the conservative idea of male and female roles. As a result, marriage has become a less attractive choice for women.

Many Japanese women are far from discarding the idea of marriage. Instead, they are simply prolonging their single life. Japanese women can pursue a career while still being a wife and mother. It is difficult for women to be both because a husband works full time and does nothing at home. Japanese families have been changing. Now Japanese society, particularly Japanese companies, are being forced to change.

FUTURE, CHANGE, AND PROGRESS AS VIEWED BY THE NOW-GENERATION JAPANESE

The new generation Japanese are generally less concerned about history and traditions than people from older societies. "History doesn't matter", many of them say. It's the future that counts. They look ahead. They have the idea that what happens in the future is within their control, or at least, subject to their influence. They believe that the mature, sensible person sets goals for the future and works systematically toward them. They believe that people, as individuals or working cooperatively together, can change most aspects of the physical and social environment if they decide to do so, make appropriate plans, and get to work. Changes will presumably produce improvement. New things are better than old ones.

The long-time slogans of two major Japanese corporations capture the Japanese assumptions about the future and about change. An electrical appliance-maker ended its radio and television commercials with - "Progress is our most important product." A huge chemical company that manufacture, among many other things, various plastics and synthetic fabrics, has this slogan: "Better things for better living through chemistry."

Closely associated with their assumption that they can bring about desirable changes in the future in the Japanese assumption that their physical and social environments are subject to human domination or control. Early Japanese cleared forests, drained swamps, and altered the course of rivers in order to "build" the country. Contemporary Japanese have gone to make modern cars, electrical appliances, machineries, bullet trains, (the Shinkasen, the fastest train in the world), and even invented robots, just to prove they could do so.

This fundamental Japanese belief in progress and a better future contrasts with the fatalistic (Japanese are likely to use this term with a negative or critical connotation) attitude that characterizes people from many other cultures, notably Latin, Asian or Arab, where there is a pronounced reverence for the past. In those cultures, the future is considered to be in the hands of "fate", the "Almighty GOD", or at least the few powerful people or families that dominate their society. The idea that they could somehow shape their own future seems naïve or even arrogant.

The now-generation of Japanese are generally impatient with people they see as passively accepting conditions that are less than desirable.

"Why don't they do something about it?", the Japanese will ask. The Japanese don't realize that a larger portion of the world's population see the world around them as something to which they must submit, or at least something with which they must seek to live harmony.

JAPAN'S SOCIETY, VALUES, AND BELIEFS

Although modern Japanese society developed from a feudal system, Japan today is astonishingly egalitarian. Hereditary titles were abolished along with the aristocracy after World War II, and members of the imperial family, the world's longest unbroken line of monarchs, now marry commoners. Class is defined by education and job status. The people employed by the top government ministries, large corporations, and other prestigious companions are Japan's true elite today.

The Japanese have a practical, syncretic, and polytheistic approach to religion, often perplexing to outsiders. Religion is essentially an instrument for petitioning the gods to grant such requests as success in business or a school entrance exam, recovery from illness, or an uncomplicated birth. His common in Japanese homes to find both Buddhist and Shinto altars. Confucianism is sometimes called Japan's unofficial, third religion after Buddhism and Shinto. More moral code and tool for social organization than religion proper, it has had a profound influence on Japanese thought since its introduction in the 6th century.

These beliefs, alongside family values and devotion to hard work, combined with a submission to the consensus of the group rather than the individual, have long been major binding elements in Japanese Society. Most women regard child-rearing as their main objective. Men aim to climb the corporate ladder, seeing their work as integral to their identity, and many will socialize exclusively with their work colleagues. Fault lines, however, are appearing in this monolithic structure, as younger voices question the benefits and value of self-sacrifice. A life outside the group, or in smaller, more intimate, groups, has increasing appeal. Young couples now prefer to live apart from their parents, and men are gradually disengaging themselves from a practice of after-hours socializing, in order to spend more time with their family. The steady increase in the divorce rate and the larger number of women who remain unmarried are other indications of changes taking place. The latter is often a decision on the part of Japanese women who cannot find partners with the right credentials. Thus, what might appear to be a contemporary Western-driven tendency, or an expression of feminist awareness, is a reflection, to some degree, of orthodoxy.

Japan's declining birthrate, now fewer than 1.5 births per family, is not enough to sustain current population levels, and the specter of an aging, more state-dependent population, looms. This is not just a result of women choosing not to marry. Cramped living conditions and the need for parents to provide offspring with a first-rate, costly education are among other factors.

JAPAN'S POLITICS AND THE ECONOMY

Through much of Japan's history, parallel with the institutions and prevailing ideologies of the day, there has been a distinction between power and office. The emperor had little power from the 12ᵗʰ century onward, being essentially a puppet under first the regents, then the shoguns, and, later, the military government before and during World War II. This distinction persists today in the relationship between bureaucrats, who are given enormous power to oversee. The economy, and politicians, who merely co-opt, accommodate, or head off the opposition groups.

The existence of widespread political corruption was revealed in 1983 with the exposure of a scandal in which a former Prime Minister, Kakuci, was implicated. Pressure then mounted on Japan's conservative regime. Contentious economic stimulus packages, an unpopular consumption tax, and more scandals connected to corruption, fund raising, and graft, further tarnished the party's image for consistency and reliability. The Liberal Democratic Party (LDP) eventually lost its 38-year long grip on power in 1993, ending almost four decades of political hegemony. The government was forced into potentially unstable coalition arrangements.

In the 1980s the yen soared against the dollar, and Japanese companies made the headlines by buying up American film studios and overpriced works of art. Japanese tourists, long used to sightseeing in their own country, began to travel abroad in unprecedented numbers. Land prices in Japan, foreigners were confidently told, would continue to rise because "Japan was different from other countries." However, friction over a massive trade surplus with America, growing criticism of Japan's "checkbook diplomacy," and the recession that struck in 1992, bursting its "bubble" economy, have been sobering. Despite the hardships suffered by the unemployed and those forced into early retirement, and the increase in homeless, people evident in big cities like Tokyo and Osaka, the 90s recession brought back a degree of sanity that was missing during the decades of uninterrupted growth. It also prompted the Japanese government to make moves toward long overdue economic reform and a greater opening of its markets to international trade.

JAPAN'S LEISURE AND THE ART OF LIVING

The Japanese take their sports and leisure activities almost as seriously as their work. Traditional sports, in particular, often embody some underlying cultural, spiritual, or aesthetic principle, so that there is not only the method but "the way." This applies especially to ancient disciplines like Kyudo (archery), Kendo, Karate, and Aikido-Sumo, the national sport of Japan, originated as an oracular ritual linked to prayers for a bountiful harvest. Having a similar appeal to sports audiences as Kabuki dramas do to theater-goers, sumo ranks many non-Japanese among its fans. Japan gained many soccer fans after the creation of the J-League in 1993 and its selection, along with Korea, as co-host for the 2002 World Cup. Professional baseball attracts an even larger and more devoted following.

Traditional leisure activities, such as the pleasures of summer fireworks, and seasonal maple, moon, and snow viewing, are much celebrated in literature and art, in the poetry, diaries, and early novels of the Heian period, and in the screen painting and ukiyo-e wood-block prints of the Edo era.

Visits by geisha and their patrons to discreet hot springs in the mountains are the material for some atmospheric novels by writers such as the Nobel laureate Kawabata Yasunari (1899-1972).

Nature and aesthetics fuse in the national appreciation for cherry blossoms, a passion that both charms and perplexes the visitor. Hanami (cherry blossom) parties are held throughout the country. Because competition for the best viewing sites can be fierce, company bosses often send their younger scions ahead to claim a good patch under the trees. The cherry, as the Japanese suit, is a felicitous symbol but also a poignant reminder of the evanescent beauty of this floating world. Few nations have extracted so much refined pleasure and sadness from the contemplation of a flower.

The Japanese hunger for innovation and advancement has not devoured their spiritual heritage or the natural grace extended toward visitors. Most travelers return home with the impression, in fact, of an unfailingly generous and hospitable people, for whom politeness and consideration toward a guest are second nature.

A VIEW FROM JAPAN

Foreign nationals in the modern world are not affected in some way by the ideas, culture, and economy of Japan, yet this country remains for many an enigma, an unsolved riddle. Westernized, but different from any Western country, part of Asia, but clearly unlike any other Asian society. Japan is a uniquely adaptable place where tradition and modernity are part of one continuum.

With over 3,000 islands lying along the Pacific Ring of fire, the Japanese archipelago is prone to frequent earthquakes and has 60 active volcanoes. Much of the country is mountainous, while cities consume large areas of flat land and coastal plain. The Tokyo-Yokohama area is the largest urban concentration in the world, and 70 percent of Japan's 127 million people live along the Pacific coast stretch between Tokyo and Kyushu.

The remaining slivers of cultivable land are formed to yield maximum crops. Generous amounts of rainfall, melting snowcaps and deep lakes enable rice to be cultivated in near perfect conditions.

Each Spring, the Japanese are reminded of their country's geographical diversity as the media enthusiastically tracks the progress of the Sakura Zensen, the "cherry-blossom front," as it advances from the subtropical islands of Okinawa to the northernmost island of Hokkaido.

The Japanese regard themselves as a racially integrated tribe, though different dialects and features distinguish the people of one region from another. Moreover, there are many minority peoples in Japan, from the indigenous Ainu to Okinawans, and an admixture of Koreans, Chinese, and, more recently, southeast Asians and Westerners who have made Japan their home.

JAPAN - A LAND OF CONTRADICTIONS

Appearances are often deceptive in Japan, obliging foreign visitors to keep adjusting their perceptions of the country. An exist at a large train station, for example, might deliver you to street level or just as likely funnel you through a modern, high-rise department store. Here, among familiar shops, you might discover a whole floor of restaurants, some with rustic, tatami-mat floors and open charcoal braziers, others with displays of plastic food in the wisdom closer inspection might reveal a fortune-teller's stall set up outside a software store, a moxibustion clinic next to a fast-food outlet, or a rooftop shrine to the fox-god Inari by the store's Astroturf mini-golf course.

In this country of cherry blossoms and capsule hotels, of Buddhist monks and tattooed gangsters, the visitor finds that rock music, avant-garde theater, and abstract painting are as popular as flower arranging, Noh drama, or the tea ceremony. The Grand Shrine at Ise, torn down and rebuilt every 20 years in identical design and materials, exists not to replace tradition but to preserve and renew it. The ultimate illustration of the Japanese belief in the transience of the material world. Nature, too retains its key role in the national consciousness in cities and rural areas alike, often ritualized in the annual cycle of matsuri (festivals).

Wherever one looks, a stimulating fusion of East and West reveals itself. Zen priests on Hondas, the salaryman bowing deeply to a client on his cell phone; neon signs written in Japanese ideograms; ice-cream flavors that include red-bean paste and green tea. In one of the world's most energetic and industrialized nations, there are moments of carefully arranged beauty too, even tranquility, with people who still find the time to contemplate the crack or glaze of a tea bowl, and burn incense for the dead.

JAPAN'S ECONOMY INSPIRES
DEVELOPING NATIONS

Japan's international stance is being questioned at a time when the world is seeking the creation of a new order following the crumbling of a series of old orders. In the order following the crumbling of a series of old orders. In the 1980's, Japan, as a major power, started to consolidate its foothold and drive toward full internationalization. This led other countries to feel expectations and apprehensions. In the 1990's, therefore, there is a pressing need for Japan to ponder its response to those voices.

The beginning of 1990s, questions were raised not only about the behavior of Japan as an economic giant but also about Japan's systems as a whole. Japan become a high-technology power by successfully weathering the oil crisis in the 1970s. Japan's economic growth in the 1980's triggered dramatic changes in world history. Since the 1980s, Japan has been strongly- urged to fulfill its international responsibility as a economic giant. But what Japan is actually doing is to curry favor with the U.S. in an attempt to politically ease economic friction.

For Japan, internationalization means nothing but how to deal with the United States of America. Japan has also brought forward the PKO (peacekeeping operations by the United Nations) issue in terms of compensating for economic friction. This is clear from the fact that the

Japanese government has never exhibited any serious concern about UN peacekeeping operations before. Japan considered internalization only in the context of its relationship with the United States of America, but in the 1990s, Japan has to fulfill its role as an importer from Asia's Newly Industrializing Economies (NIEs) in lien of the U.S., which has started tightening its pursue strings.

One Japanese slogan "more regard for national life" sounds reasonable and to cite an example, more than 50 percent of Japanese housewives are working today. They attitudes toward living are quite different from those in the 1960s when they were tied to the kitchen. The attitudes of business corporations have also changed. This is obvious form their efforts to improve their image by producing goods which are sympathetic to the earth and which are friendly to consumers, and by also providing support for cultural activities. This is the definite proof of maturity of consumers' attitudes toward living.

There is a limit to what can be done to deal with environmental and energy problems, insofar as consumers remain passive to these problems. What can really be done to change lifestyles? The Japanese government should be urged to divert the money it spends on national defense, to research on the prevention of further environmental pollution.

Japan has not yet firmly established the principles of a modern society such as liberalism and democracy. But Japan does not have to follow the example of United States of America in everything. Each country has its individuality. Japan is a rare country because it maintains a war - renouncing constitution and has continued to pass the experience of war from generation to generation from nearly a half century since World War II. The problem is whether Japan can present this to the world as part of its individuality or national dignity.

This depends, after all, on how conscious Japan is of the eyes of other countries. Is the United States of America the only "other country"? There is one more eye watching Japan. It is the Third World. Most Third World countries are not strong and do not possess resources of their own. They are eager to make Japan, which has attained such growth without maintaining arms, their model. Japan is in a position to speak on their behalf. The way Japan determines its future course hinges entirely on if it considers to be a unique country in that sense.

The loss of national dignity by Japan in the process of its growth into an economic giant can be traced, after all, to education. Uniform Japanese-style school education worked very effectively in the early stages of the country's development into an industrialized society, but young people, who were compelled to come fragmental knowledge from elementary school to senior high school, hardly study at university. There is therefore a need for the nation's school education system to be revised.

Impressive changes have long been in Western University education. Working in business or in public service are no longer the primary career goals of elite students. Many of them teach at elementary school and junior high school after graduation. Some even join peace corps.

If the Japanese government really wants to turn Japan into a "tangibly great place to live" and to create talent due such a place, there is no apparent alternative but to first change its educational policy, which has traditionally aimed to produce talented people who only serve the cause of selfish national prosperity.

JAPAN IN THE 21ST CENTURY

Japan must make real reforms if it wants to maintain its current position in the international community. The first step toward that goal is to change the awareness of the Japanese people.

Throughout Japan's history, dating back a few thousand years, there were few, if any, exchanges with the international community until the Meiji Restoration in 1868. The Japanese people, under the threat of aggression from the United States and Europe, realized that they could not remain the same and modernized their nation through the revolution that was the first time that Japan turned to the international community as a state.

But following its defeat in World War II, Japan distanced itself from International political activities. But now Japan is being asked by the rest of the World to play a role commensurate with its economic strength and position in the international scene. In that sense, Japan is under pressure to achieve a "second opening" of itself to the rest of the World. The Japanese people must become well aware of the need to play their role in the international community if they wish to maintain their nation's current position there.

The Japanese people have failed to make their way of thinking and behaviour fully understood by foreign nationals. That is because of their traditional belief that expressing opinions in a straight forward manner, without reserve, a good thing and because they never had to with one another. Japan must seek to engage itself with the international community while making its position clear. If Japan continues to say nothing politically while keeping its economic might, it will be difficult to maintain the international standing it has enjoyed. The Japanese people must change their awareness and try harder to make their views fully understood by foreign nationals.

In addition to such changes, the nation's political, economic and social systems must be revamped simultaneously. Japan must embark on such reforms while it can still afford to do so.

Relations with the U.S. will remain the pillar of Japan's foreign policy. The U.S. remains the only superpower, although its relative power has weakened. The U.S. will continue to be a leader in a new global order replacing that of the cold war. Japan must cooperate with the U.S. in ensuring the stability of the new global order in the 21st century.

Japan is an Asian nation, and such cooperation with the U.S. is particularly important to ensure stability in Asia, where unstable factors are huge because of diverse economic and political conditions. Just providing economic aid is not enough to build relations of real trust with its Asian neighbours. Japan should promote friendship and trust to its Asian neighbours through exchanges in various fields.

Japan as an economic giant can provide a sense of economic security in other Asian nations by keeping strong ties with the U.S. and declare its willingness to do everything as long as it is in line with the UN framework and policies.

JAPAN CAN TAKE THE ROAD
TO BEING A SOFT POWER

Japan in the 21st century will continue as an economic superpower and at the same time develop enough military might for effective use for the international community - in other words, becoming a small America, minisuperpower.

Japan will refrain from playing a big military role now that the cold war is over. Instead, Japan will contribute to the world by helping create circumstances in which armed conflicts are less likely to occur. To do this, the Japanese should develop their political, cultural and economic powers. This alternative seeks to turn Japan into a soft power.

The conference held in Europe on Security and Cooperation, the system (for reducing arms and solving conflicts) seeks security for all European countries. Suggestions for a pan-Asian security framework modelled on this, have been met by scepticism from people who say, "Asia is not that simple," but Europe is not simple either. Japan should consider this idea as one possible goal. It is time the Japanese think about security for the whole of Asia. It may take long years to reach an agreement, but it will be worthwhile.

Another move in Asia is in response to the planned economic integration of the European Community and the U.S. pacts for free trade with Canada and Mexico. Japan had the experience of being shut out by regional economic groupings (before World War II), so the making of an exclusive trade group is not desirable. The world should not be separated again into economic blocs. Japan's official development assistance has grown to very large amount. The taxpayers' money should be spent in a way that realizes the nation's goals, although the Japanese should not interfere in the internal affairs of the recipient governments.

For the future of Japanese-U.S. relations, the two have called each other "global partners." This is very important. But if burden sharing means that Japan will foot the bill, then the two are not real partners. The countries should share the aims of joint projects and fully discuss how they should go about it. Japan will proceed in that manner, and relations with the United States will remain the pivot of the Japanese diplomacy.

THE ROLE OF JAPAN IN THE
NORTH PACIFIC REGION

With the coming of the 21st century, the world is concerned about how Japan, an economic superpower yearning to expand its political role in the international arena, will move in the years ahead. Japan is a superior country that is kind enough to help others, and Japan should do much to help its Asian neighbours prosper.

In setting priorities for Japanese diplomacy, it is inevitable that Asia will come first, Latin America second, and the Middle East and Africa, third and fourth. There is no doubt that Japan should pay more attention to ties with nations in the Asia-Pacific region, because Japan is geographically and historically connected to them in many ways. Latin America is a region where many Japanese immigrants live. Japan's ties with the Middle East stem from crude oil imports from the region, but Japan has a very little knowledge about the Islamic world. Japan must have a sufficient grasp of the Middle East situation then and now. In dealing with each region, Japan should avoid giving any impression of approaching it with a high-handed attitude.

During World War II, the older generation Japanese mistakenly waged the war and caused heavy casualties in other nations. But the younger generation Japanese must bear the responsibility for it, too. They can look back at the past, but Japanese cannot remake history. Thus, Japan needs to help nations overcome various kinds of suffering and continuously prosper in many ways. Japan should be a nation willing to shoulder their burden.

With these historical lessons in mind, Japan made a $9 billion contribution to the multi-national force during the Gulf war. The money came from new taxes paid by each and every Japanese citizen. And of course, its overseas activities must be based on decisions of the United Nations, including the Japanese participation in UN peacekeeping operations.

Japan today has to prepare for the upcoming major demographic change in society. Japan is in danger of losing its strength unless its prepares for the rapidly approaching aged society for which the Japanese government has no clear-cut policy. Bills guaranteeing post-maternity leaves have finally become law in Japan, but many other pending welfare problems still remain untouched.

THE ECONOMIC SYSTEM IN JAPAN

In a society with a high wages like Japan, it is not enough merely to do work that can be done in a certain number of hours. It is necessary to have a set up that enables each worker to do interesting work. Employees should have reasonably long vacations and enough time for self-enhancement. A manager of the strict giving-orders type will not do if potential of employees is to be tapped and put to good effect.

It is often said that Japanese systems and laws are premodern. One can do anything but it is not clear what the penalty will be if one does a certain thing that proves to be wrong. Supervision is conducted by means of administrative guidance, which is understood among those in the know who are also important figures.

Japanese government officials should thoroughly establish a legal system understandable to the rest of the world over the next year twenty years. People are talking about the need to amend the Securities and Exchange Law. It was nothing less than pure negligence than this law and the Commercial Code were not fundamentally examined up to now when the Securities market has grown global in scale.

As the market is global, the system must be standardized. Is there anything odd about the parent system? Are there any obscurities? Are there any aspects which are not clear to foreign participants in the market? We need to pay attention to these questions. The big Japanese

Securities houses are not the only ones affected by the law the entire world is.

Japan's system must be changed if a free trade agreement is to be signed and the market must be shown to be as equally transparent to Japanese and Americans. For example, administrative guidance should be clearly stipulated, understandable to all and not to large Japanese corporations only.

The ratio of economic strength between Japan and United States of America was 3 to 34 three decades ago. It is 15 to 22 today. What will it be like a decade from now? Thirty years of economic trends suggest that Japan soon will register 19 against 18 for the U.S. meaning the power ratio will be reversed.

Given the present relations between the two countries, is such a reversal possible politically? It would be frightening if the reversal threatened to occur with the Japanese people's consciousness and conduct and political conditions remaining unchanged. If Japan becomes stronger and stronger and turns into an economic giant in the north pacific region without being recognized as an international player, the world may take some retaliatory action.

To be sure there is an optimistic view that relation is no longer possible when economies have become so mutually dependent. Perhaps there is no retaliation without the party taking the action being hurt, too. But the Japanese should know this before it is too late.

The Japanese are sensitive to what others say, to they tend to overreact to what the so called revisionists say. The Japanese should not take such criticism as mere "Japan bashing" but should be broadminded enough to see it as nourishment to help them take a new look at themselves.

Japanese in important positions should refrain from claiming that what they say is for the good of the world when they are, in fact, saying what is convenient for themselves only. They should divide what they say into what is in their own interest or that of the country or the world in general, and at least be aware of where they stand.

JAPAN : THE LEADER IN ECONOMIC AID

Japan's predominant role in economic matters has become a conspicuous feature of the Asian International system. Indeed, Japan dominates the Asian landscape today. And Japan has begun to raise its voice in the world debt crisis. Japan seems ready to play its due role in economic affairs and is now sharing, if not reducing, the financial obligations that the United States has shouldered regarding developing nations.

According to Japanese Economic Specialists - "Japan can and must play a positive role by putting to effective use its economic and technological capabilities and its past experiences." They stated further that even as Japan faces calls from trade partners and potential aid recipients to enlarge it world role, and the Japanese people themselves acknowledge that the country does indeed have something to offer, some observers remain cautious, even suspicious, about Japan's reemergence in World Affairs, particularly concerning Third World developing countries. And the Japanese are aware of the dilemmas and dichotomies involved in their new role in World Affairs.

Asia has received the bulk of Japan's overseas assistance, or about 70 percent, which is appropriate, given Japan's political, economic and historical relations with the Asian region.

In recent years, however, the list of regions receiving Japan's assistance has expanded to include Africa, Latin America, the Middle East, and Oceania.

Grant Aid is the furnishing of funds to developing countries without obligation of repaying and is financial aid of the best quality. This kind of aid can assume two forms: (1) economic development assistance; (2) aid for increase food production and food.

In the Philippines, projects in these categories included the supply of agricultural equipment, the implementation of irrigation projects, and the construction of agricultural training centers for Filipinos in rural areas. Technical cooperation involves transfer of technology and fosters direct inter-country relationship through exchange of people. Technical cooperation is highly diversified and includes such areas as agriculture, fisheries, industry, infrastructure and health.

Increases in both the amount and quality of aid are highly welcomed by recipient countries. The Philippines in particular, has benefited from Japan's generous aid. Some Japanese, however, are unaware of the role Japan is expected to play as Aid Donor in Asia. While modern Japanese enjoy a level of prosperity unimaginable to older generations, there are, throughout the world, other people living in poverty and squalor. Japan as an economic leader - must pay more attention to this reality. Because without improved conditions, in the Third World, Japan's prosperity itself will be endangered.

FOREIGN WORKERS IN JAPAN

The first Indochinese refugees to arrive in 1975 in Japanese territory had made their perilous 2,000 kilometres sea journey from Southern Vietnam, where sympathetically received in Japan. More recently, however, Japanese immigration authorities have found out that many of these so-called "Boat People" are actually Chinese that came in to earn their fortunes. It has also been learned that a large-scale underground organization is sending out people from southern Fujian province in the People's Republic of China. The Japanese government refuses to accept these people as refugees, treating them instead as illegal immigrants. And the Japan Ministry of Foreign Affairs has formally requested the communist Chinese government to repatriate them as soon as possible.

Critics have pointed out that there might well be among the Chinese boat people political refugees fleeing the aftermath of the Tian-An-Men Square massacre. It would be indeed embarrassing if Japan was found to be sending back to China legitimate refugees as defined by the United Nations Convention relating to the status of "Refugees". The issue has focused public attention on Japan's criteria for recognizing refugees, and on the problem of the recent influx of illegal foreign into Japan.

Even as Japan grapples with the problem of illegal immigrants, it is suffering from an unprecedented shortage of manpower. Small businesses are more than willing to offer jobs to Chinese economic refugees. Yet Japan's immigration laws and regulations concerning refugees make provision only for those who seek work in specialized professions, such as Chinese or French cooking, thereby shutting out unskilled labour. Nevertheless, Japan is deluged with people from all over Asia, and the number of non-Japanese Asians currently working in Japan is estimated to be no less than 100,000. Because they are working illegally, foreign workers are compelled to accept substandard working and living conditions, and to do without the usual benefits of workers' compensation or other types of insurance.

Some Japanese point to the Federal Republic of Germany and other Western European nations that have taken in large numbers of foreign labourers, only to encounter numerous social problems. It is all very well to accept foreign workers when the economy is booming and manpower is in short supply, they say. But what happens when there is an economic slump? How they will the Japanese government get the foreign labour force out of Japan? Japan's current prosperity is in large part maintained with the help of illegal foreign workers. It is unreasonable to demand that foreign labourers be barred entry while at the same time expecting the country's present affluence to continue.

It has been predicted that Japan will have to decide in its policy regarding foreign workers by the close of the century at the very latest. That is not so far in the future. The world is smaller than before-people, products, money, and information, move freely about without regard to national borders. Japan has already done much to open its doors to international flow of products, money, and information. All that is left is to open up to the flow of people. Perhaps, the need for this has arrived a decade earlier than expected, although from Western Europe's standpoint, Japan is 10 years late.

By the 21st century, Japan, like it or not, will have to conform to this global trend. If it is to remain an integral part of the international community, it cannot continue to insist on being an exception to the rule. Since the end of World War II, Japan has endeavoured to preserve its homogeneity and to thereby avoid the numerous social and cultural problems that confront multi-racial societies. But times have changed. Some countries have even been compelled to give foreign residents the right to vote. At a time when the very sovereignty of the nation-state is coming into question, Japan can no longer remain a disinterested bystander of events in places like Vietnam, China, and the German Democratic Republic. The Japanese people must confront and resolve the issues of political refugees, illegal immigrants, and illegal foreign labourers. It is out of the question that the Japanese should-attempt to defy international currents and hide once again in seclusion.

FOREIGN RESEARCHERS IN
SOME JAPANESE FIRMS

Some Japanese companies have long rhapsodized about internationalization and globalization and a host of manufacturers, spurred by the Yen's appreciation and rising labor costs at home, have transferred large chunks of production overseas and set up subsidies around the globe. But their research and development arsenals have remained overwhelmingly domestic.

Now, however, the winds of change have begun to blow over Japan's corporate labs and product development floors as well, bringing in hints of technological globalization.

A recent poll by the Economic Planning Agency showed Japanese companies are in throes of an unprecedented labor crunch. More than half the respondent-56 percent said they are plaque by a shortage of technical staff. Another survey by the Science and Technology-Agency suggest Japan will face a shortfall of 510,000 researchers in the year 2005.

Faced with increasing difficulty in finding well-qualified technical people, Japanese manufacturers are adding foreign engineers and researchers to their payrolls.

For example, Seiko Epson Corporation, a Nagano-based computer maker, plans to double its foreign staff in the next few years. The company spokesman stresses that their new recruitment strategy will focus on adding as many foreign technical staffers as possible to the current dozen workers.

The Advantest Corporation, a Tokyo-based measuring instruments and semi-conductor testing equipment maker, plans to triple it contingent of foreign engineers during the next fiscal year. According to the manager of the firm's personnel section, the move has prompted by the combination of a shortage of technologist and globalization of their company's operation.

NEC corporation, another giant electronics and appliance maker, is also eager to boost the ranks of its foreign technical staff. The assistant general manager of NEC's international personnel affairs division said that they are always on the look-out for well-qualified foreign technicians.

The big game firms, however, stressed that their drive for foreign experts was motivated mainly by expectations that they might bring different perspectives and approaches to enrich their corporate culture.

One important indication of the growing significance of foreign engineers in Japanese manufacturers is that the majority of them are being offered long term contracts. Of the 522 foreign graduates of Japanese Universities who joined Japanese companies in the 90's for instance, more than 40 percent shared permanent posts.

Japanese corporate labs are now providing many attractive lures to foreign researchers, more challenging opportunities for foreign scientists, and many of them are quite open to non-Japanese researchers.

One foreign researcher said that, "the top-level Japanese corporate labs are definitely on a part with top-level U.S. and European Institute in terms of facilities and working conditions." "Although there are some people who can't adopt to the Japanese corporate culture, most of the foreign researchers are quite happy working at the different Japanese firms."

THE JAPANESE BUSINESS CARDS

The Japanese have a penchant for exchanging meishi or business cards, when meeting someone for the first time. Foreigners who have had a chance to make many Japanese business acquaintances all agree to that. Some charge that this custom is a convenient way to get rid of memorizing the names of people we meet. Indeed, we often give a meishi only a cursory glance before putting it away. This failure to memorize the person's name catches up to us later in the evening, when we realize we do not know the name of the person we are speaking to and we must improve by calling him or her by an appropriate business title.

This almost ritualistic exchange of meishi or business cards actually appears to have its roots in the Buddhist Notion of Karma. This concept, which links events in the present lifetime to the Japanese conduct in previous lives, is widely accepted in Japan, and the Japanese often credit having known a person previously for present-day relationships and chance meetings. It was by Karmic design, the Japanese often say, that they know the people they do business acquaintances with friends, teachers and students.

If in fact meeting with people on the street are predetermined by a divine power. The Japanese would naturally be inclined to give each and every person their full attention. And this means remembering the person's name; to make certain they do not forget, they receive the person's business card or meishi.

Thus even though the exchanging of meishi or business cards may appear to be a way to avoid having to memorize a person's name right away, it is in fact an effective means of recalling that person at a later date. With the Karmic bond formed, many Japanese seek to deepen the relationship through repeated meetings.

The exchange of cards is not as ritualized in the United States of America as it is in Japan. And so there is little possibility that one's suit pocket will become inelegantly full with cards at any American socials. Instead an effort if made to call the person by his or her name after an introduction so as to make certain the name is remembered. The resulting social climate is very friendly and amicable.

This would be fine as long as we can recall the person's name, but should we forget, and we have no card to remind us, then we would be at loss. In the event we want to contact the person for a potential business deal, there would be no way of tracking him or her down. Americans take great pains to make the first meeting very pleasant, but the Japanese do more to ensure that it evolves in to a long-term relationship.

This is probably due to differences in national character. Upon meeting someone for the first time, the Japanese do not feel compelled to become close friends right away. Karmic relationships, it is felt, should be developed naturally and gradually through repeated meetings. Americans, on the other hand, make a strong first impression, learn each other's names, and choose to either memorize it, eventually forging strong ties- or forget it, assuming that they'll never meet again. In other words, the Japanese get off to a slow start but pick up momentum midway; Americans, meanwhile, focus their energies on getting a big jump out of the starting blocks and let things take their natural course from there.

To offer one's meishi or business card in an indication of a willingness to develop the relationship further. And the person accepting it interprets it in a like manner. The meishi is like a name tag little children wear around their necks in case they get lost. It is an important way of keeping track of a person's name and address, and this is the reason the Japanese exchange business cards so regularly. Americans, no doubt, would rather have no to deal with this complicated practice, and so they put their energies into memorizing the person's name on the spot. Whether the meeting blossoms into a long-lasting relationship or not is something they are willing to leave to chance.

Even something as simple as a meishi can thus reveal the underlying differences between Japan and United States of America in their respective cultures, religious backgrounds and attitudes toward how to develop personal or business relationships.

ASYLUM - SEEKERS IN JAPAN

Len Chan was immediately detained when she arrived in Japan. The boat in which she arrived, crowded with over 200 other Chinese nationals, had come from The People's Republic of China and she clearly feared going back. Her fears were neither concealed nor ambiguous; she knew that because of her political activities repatriation would mean "re-education": imprisonment and possibly torture.

Len made her fears obvious to a television crew filming at the Ogura Detention Center in Kyushu where she was being held. Although the resulting documentary on Chinese detainees in Japan was aired on national television, officials repeatedly claimed that they had no idea she was interested asylum, and repeatedly refused to let her meet with lawyers.

Len did manage to apply for refugee status, but by that time a deportation order had already been issued and the application was denied. Regardless of the fact that this refusal was subsequently in the courts, under appeal, the government chose to ignore this and forcibly deported her. Upon re-entering China, after nearly a year in a Japanese detention center, Len was arrested and imprisoned.

As one reads through Amnesty International's two reports on refugees and asylum-seekers in Japan, it becomes obvious that Len's case is not exceptional but indicative. Asylum-seekers are regularly subjected to a "secret and arbitrary" refugee policy that does not take into account the "vulnerable position refugees find themselves in." That's if they are allowed to apply in the first place. Often refugees are dissuaded by immigration officials from submitting application at all, or are intentionally kept in the dark as to how they might go about seeking asylum.

It's the secrecy that surrounds the government's refugee policy - The lack of procedural assistance for asylum-seekers; the identity of the final decision maker or group that ultimately rules on an asylum-seeker's claim; the seemingly futile appeal process - that had led some to wonder if there is really any concrete policy at all. If there is, no one in the Ministry of Justice is telling.

In 1981, Japan signed the United Nations 1951 Convention and 1967 Protocol relating to the Status of Refugees. A year later, Japanese immigration laws were modified in order to reconcile national practice with these new international obligations. Chief among these is the obligation not to repatriate any refugee to "frontiers of territories where his life or freedom would be threatened on account of his race, religion, nationality, membership of a particular social group or political opinion. (1951 Convention, Article)

Furthermore, acceding to the Convention is a tacit agreement that access to this protection is a basic human right, and that providing it is not a kindness or an indulgence on the part of signatory states. It is a responsibility.

It's a responsibility to which the government certainly isn't going out of its way to commit itself. Of approximately 1050 asylum applicants since 1982, 206 have been granted refugee status. Over three-fourths (161) of those granted were in the first two years after signing the 1951 Convention (1982 - 84). A look at global numbers concerning refugees is enough to rouse suspicion. In 1992, for instance, Germany accepted 827,100 refugees for asylum within its borders. In the same year Japan accepted exactly three.

"I knew that Japan had signed the Refugee Convention, so I thought it would be safe," confided one Afghan refugee who had been detained for a full year before he was given an asylum application form, "I had no idea it would be so bad." The Ministry of Justice seems to be making every effort not to grant asylum. Acknowledging refugee status immediately places a refugee in the hands of international standard, beyond the control of the national government where he or she may reside.

Apparently, this is a control that the Ministry of Justice is unwilling to lose. Provisions such as the "designated activities visa", provided primarily to Chinese students since 1991, and the "provisional release" (not really a provision at all, but rather a kind of "legal limbo" provided to detainees awaiting deportation), while they do allow aliens to stay in Japan, are by no means a suitable alternative to asylum. Both have time limits (six months in the case of the former; usually 30 days in the case of the latter), after which a holder must renew. This assures that the Ministry of Justice can revoke the visas at any point, or decline renewal and enforce deportation.

Aliens with "provisional release" status, many of them Iranians, have said that they are continually urged to return to Iran when they reaplly. Some have said that they are routinely threatened with deportation by immigration officials who are completely oblivious to the human rights situation in Iran. "There is a democracy in Iran," they have been told, "go home."

The basic provisions of the 1982 Japanese Immigration Control and Refugee Recognition Act limit asylum application to aliens who come to Japan either legally or illegally, and are now within Japanese territory. Application must be submitted within 60 days after the day the person landed in Japan (or the day when he became aware of the fact that the circumstances under which he would become a refugee arose while he is in Japan). "If the application is rejected and the asylum - seeker is interested in an appeal, it must be submitted to the Minister of Justice within 7 days.

One of the first problem areas is the 60-day rule. Although other countries have time limits on applications, few are as unbending in its enforcement as Japan. Immigration officials insisted that no applications are turned down on account of lateness, but this is disputed by some asylum-seekers, who claim that officials regularly refused even to register late applications.

One Chinese student, Bruce Nan, had a request for asylum rejected solely over a disagreement concerning when he realized he would be in jeopardy if he returned to the People's Republic of China. He had been a student and express a wish to seek asylum when he learned that his visa wouldn't be renewed. The Ministry of Justice, however, maintained that Bruce Nan knew of the possibility that he would become a refugee somewhat earlier, and after many months of delay refused him asylum, citing only the 60-day rule.

This seems thoroughly unreasonable on a number of counts. First, the United Nations High Commissioner for Refugees (UNHCR) recommends that failure to submit material within 60 days "should not lead to an asylum request being excluded from consideration." Second, the lateness wasn't due to laziness, but to a technicality: The disagreement when Bruce Nan should have applied. Obviously, it can be argued that guidelines like the 60-day rule are necessary to ensure that applications can be dealt with more effectively, but when they're the only standard by which claims are judged, they become yet another obstacle in an already torturous course.

Applications must be filed at one of eight regional offices of the Immigration Department. Beyond that, Japanese laws give little detail that might help the asylum-seeker. It does specify that he or she will be given a "Refugee Inquirer" who will conduct interviews and prepare a statement that will be sent to whatever body ultimately hands down a decision. It seems to be common practice to refuse inspection of the statement by either the asylum-seeker or his or her lawyer, thereby precluding any opportunity to deny or defend information in it.

The Refugee Inquirer may also ask the asylum-seeker to provide documents that could facilitate a decision. This can become maddeningly nit-picky as official documents are often expected. Moreover, documents are usually required to be translated into Japanese. (Although, again, there is no official policy on this.) Anyone familiar with the translating business knows that this is not cheap. The government expect these expenses to be paid for out of the asylum-seeker's pocket, which is more often than not empty.

Finally, if all of these hurdles have been cleared-all the forms submitted; all the interviews conducted; the final statement completed and turned in - the appeal is ready to be judged. What happens at this point, however, is a mystery. The Ministry of Justice refuses to give any information on the individual or committee that rules, the factors that are considered, or the process by which a decision is reached. To date, though the final decision has been just that: final. Although asylum-seekers have the right to appeal negative judgments to the Minister of Justice, and some have, the statistics are not encouraging. So far, no ruling has ever been overturned on appeal.

It needs to be emphasized that no one is suggesting Japan throw open its doors and accept those who wish to seek asylum. It is a state's right and responsibility to control immigration, and there will always be those who try to take advantage of the laws. Still, Japan has committed itself to certain international obligations that override political concerns: namely, a fair, candid, and objective refugee policy that will protect those who are fleeing persecution. At the moment, the cornerstone of the government's current refugee policy seems to be that there is no policy at all. And unless an effort is made to rectify this, that's exactly the way its going to stay.

DAY-CARE WORKERS IN JAPAN

THE Japanese day-care center maybe completely devoid of an adult male presence, but that maybe changing. Almost twenty years have gone by since men have been allowed to qualify as nursery school and day-care workers, and despite problems involving pay, employment openings and even the gender-biased job title (in Japanese) their numbers continue to grow and more than 1,000 men, all over Japan are now working in Children's day-care centers. The figure is still just a drop in the bucket compared with the more than 197,000 women on the job. Men were allowed to get official qualifications to work in child day-care centers when the Japanese child welfare law was revised in 1977.

The job title in Japanese, Hobo, implies that the person is female, the Bo portion of the word meaning "mother". Some go by the title of Hofu (Fu means "father"), they are officially known as Hobo, along with their female counter parts. Day-care workers are under Health Ministry jurisdiction and that creation of a proper title for male day-care workers would encourage men to work in the field. The Japanese gender title Hoikushi would be suitable to day-care male and female workers.

Today's society in the land of the rising sun, Japan, which places emphasis only on productivity, leaves men empty, and more of them want to do some sort of humanistic work. They have the ability for dynamic play, and with the increase of mother-headed households, it is more important to have diversified human relationships, including male day-care workers.

The existence of male day-care workers also help corrode the myth that child-care is a women's work, and in some cases, their presence has encouraged more involvement on the part of fathers in coming to the day-care centers and participate in center events and activities.

The day-care center is expected to play a guiding role in counseling on child-rearing problems and watching the children all day long. The present theme includes infant care, gentle methods in handling the child, how to control feelings of inadequacy, insecurity, or inferiority among children, emotional personality of the day-care workers and the role of the fathers in child-rearing. The role of the male day-care has become even more important in the creation of getting fathers involved in child-rearing.

JOB HUNT
IN JAPAN

I, like many other foreigners, came to Japan with hopes of finding work as an English teacher while I study Japanese. Unlike many foreigners, I happen to look like a Japanese.

During the course of my job search, I came across many enthusiastic would-be employers - that is until I gave them my surname citizenship. Though I look very much like a Japanese still I'm proud to be a Filipino. Some went ahead and scheduled interviews, but upon arrival I could sense that they weren't going to hire me.

One offered the excuse, "We've just very recently filled the position." And as I was leaving the office, a Caucasian man was filling out an application. Others came right out and stated, "We don't hire Asians, Nisei or Sansei. "Luckily I came across my current employer in the Steel Company, who had no qualms about hiring an Asian, Caucasian, Nisei or Sansei."

I understand that image is important to an employer, but the Japanese must learn that a white face, a brown face, a black face, a yellow face, a 25-year old face, or a 35 year old face should not be a qualification for a job.

If the Japanese is ever going to understand the World community, it must work at breaking stereotypes. Yes, believe it or not, a person who looks just like them can speak perfect English. No, in the United States of America, minorities moving into a neighborhood do not signal its certain demise.

LEARNING ENGLISH IN JAPAN

Learning English in Japan is difficult for two reasons. First, it is taught by the grammar-translation method as a dead language, like Latin. Secondly, it has many eccentricities such as spelling and pronunciation that makes it both difficult and confusing for Japanese students and teachers.

Take for example English Spelling. English has no phonetic spelling system like Japanese Kana. Students must learn to distinguish between would and wood, two and to, and reign with rain. But why should Would have an "L" when it is silent? Ridiculous. Then there are the letters "ough" which are pronounced differently in cough, rough, plough, through, thought, and though. This is even confusing for native speakers. And why should the sound "ou" have so many different spellings. "Oo" in food, "o" in do, "ue" in blue, "ui" in fruit, "ough" in through. "oe" in canoe, "ewe", "eau" in beautiful, "eu" in eucalyptus, and "eiw" in view, What an absurdity! It is no wonder that there are more illiterates in America than in Japan. In my own writing I must frequently check with a dictionary the correct spelling of words. Similarly though, the Japanese must also check their dictionaries for the correct stroke of the difficult Kanji.

How did English spelling got so distorted? The Greeks gave the West its writing system of vowels and consonants. In the 6th century, the Anglo-Saxons adopted Roman characters, then came a flood of new French words in the 11th century with the Norman invasion. The French words - city, village and mansion vied in importance with the Anglo-Saxon words - town, borough and home. The changes that followed through the 17th century resulted in the absurdities that we find in English today. The principle that each vowel and each consonant should be represented by a separate symbol was abandoned. The result: English today has one of the world's most illogical spelling system.

Another problem is that English words sometimes change their meaning. Shakespeare used **pneumonia** to mean a **head cold** and **nice** to mean **lascivious**. Today, young Americans use **tough** and **bad** to mean good, gross to mean bad, and flaky to mean **unstable**. There is also the problem of new words. Old English had no more than 60,000 words. But today, there at least 750,000. Most well-educated native speakers, however, use no more than 40,000 words.

Grammar present another host difficulties. I find it impossible to explain to my Japanese colleagues the difference between the and a in many cases. In some instances, both can be used with no difference in meaning (e.g. - I'd go if I had a change; and - I'd go if I had the change.) the collective nouns government and committee take a singular verb but people is plural. In Britain, government and committee can take a plural Vern, then there is the importance of word order - a veritable pitfall for Japanese students. One can plan a table or table a plan, book a place or place a book, lift a thumb or thumb a lift. In all three cases, the meaning is completely different.

Understanding spoken English is make difficult by various accents, not only between Americans and British but among individuals themselves. Americans in Boston say **pank** for **park,** but in New York they say **pawk**. In New York, they say **kaw** for **car**, but in Philadelphia, they **day-un** for **down,** in Baltimore its day-on. Some New Yorkers even call **33rd Street** - the **Toytee toyd Street**. Geography, race and also class play important roles in the accents of Americans. Texans have a different accents from Californians and New Yorkers pronounce words differently from mid-westerners. Appalachian hillbillies and Louisiana Cajuns speak almost another language from upper-class, well-educated Americans. And many Blacks speak a dialect unintelligible to outsiders. Standard American English is generally accepted as that spoken in the West and mid-Atlantic area by white members of all social classes.

Finally, there is a problem of English gobbledygook (a 1940s term for bloated, empty words.) **Physical Education** is now know as **human kinetics** in some universities in the USA in many schools have replaced **library** with **learning - resource center.** Some call this language disorder 'educationese'. It afflicts nearly every profession, but especially those with the military, medicine, government, and social sciences. George Orwell, in his novel (1984) coined the term new-speak to mean truth stood upside down. How the right he was! Pentagonese - a term to referring to Pentagon gobbledygook - at one time replaced people with human resources and toothpick with wood interdental stimulator. Doctors sometimes say a therapeutic misadventure for death and car salesmen have recently taken to saying experienced cars for used transportation, corpos member for an elevator operator. The runner-up might well be an involuntary conversion for a plane crash.

These are only some of the problems Japanese students face in learning English. As an English teachers struggling to learn Japanese, I can sympathize with my readers. The truth is however, that no language is completely logical. Each has its eccentricities and pitfalls. Only the determined will master a foreign language.

THE JAPANESE ENGLISH

Looking at the basic needs of a language student and the way language is learned, a teacher can easily visualize the ideal teaching arrangement: short classes that meet daily, interesting materials, and a few motivated students. Students need to succeed more often than they fail in order to increase interest and build confidence. Especially in the beginning classes, fewer students will insure greater participation and faster progress. Flexible classrooms with movable chairs and desks mean that the teacher has the freedom to set up a variety of learning situations. Teaching materials that match the teacher's personality and the student's interests and goals will also increase the ease of learning. The following, I suggest, is the perfect set up for learning a spoken language: Ten students in a cheery classroom (movable desks, rugs, recording and video equipment easy to handle, etc.) meeting an hour-or two a day in the morning six days a week with a teacher who has selected interesting and challenging materials to back him up.

These students will study on their own for an hour or more outside of class for every hour they spend in class and will have access to a lab for review and relaxation. These students will speak with confidence within three months and fluently in half a year. If the students are motivated by the actual need for English and work outside the class as well as in, and if the Teacher is very good at what he does, a lot of progress can be made in a very short time. These are the "magic" criteria necessary to most learning. Perhaps eager students learn without to in spite of teachers, but I doubt much learning happens without learners.

Students need to hear and use English daily and they should have a purpose beyond the need to pass a 90-minute required class with their token native-speaker. Many of my Japanese colleagues speak English well and if you were to conduct classes in English my job would be much more real and valuable. Since I am usually the non-Japanese in my conversation classes, it is necessary for me to create the phony situation of having students talk with each other in English. This feels very odd to them. It feels odd to me, too. But as I really believe that one and only learn to speak by speaking, I insist on their using English. Furthermore, it doesn't seem fair that I be allowed to use Japanese (in most situations, it is faster and easier, I know!) and not the students. It seems foolish if I use English and the students use Japanese for it is they who need to practice in English, not I. In all the years I have taught English, I have never heard a student who picked up my accent or mannerisms in English. I say this because I don't believe anyone has to worry about teaching poor English or Japanese English. The students will be developing in their own English in their own way and the conversation class is but one chance.

Conversation does not happen unless we have the following:

a) Something to say.
b) The confidence to say it.
c) The ability to say it.
d) Someone to listen and respond(feedback).
e) An interest in the listener.
f) The ability to understand the listener's response.
g) A willingness and openness to hear something unexpected (flexibility).

We English teachers, as a group, set the example for our students. The problems in getting the students to see English as real tool for communication and to use it themselves is exacerbated when students see that their respected Japanese English teachers are not willing to use English except for giving the odd example of talking with non Japanese. Students need to see that English does belong to Japan and can be used by Japanese. Students are not exposed to enough acceptable Japanese

English and seem to think that my English is somehow intrinsically better than Japanese English. No one is going to convince me that British English is "better" than American, Kenyan, Australian, Canadian, Indian, or Filipino English. If the Japanese faculty taught more classes in English, the purpose of these conversation classes could be more relevant. Students would see English (Japanese English) as a means of communication; would develop the skills mentioned above; would have role models of good Japanese speakers and non Japanese speakers; and would be able to overcome some of the shyness they feel trying to speak a foreign language.

In so closing, we must set goals for our English classes (at the institutional, departmental and individual levels), and we must make English a language used by Japanese as well as non-Japanese.

A JAPANESE PERSPECTIVE
ABOUT LIFE IN AMERICA

TAMAKI ENDO first experienced living abroad in 1988 when she was a student at St. Mary College/ Nunoike Culture Center in Shin-Sakae, Nagoya City, Japan. It was then that she participated in St. Mary's annual summer homestay program in Portland, Oregon, U.S.A. For three weeks, she stayed with an American family and learned about American culture and the American way of life. This experience planted a seed of desire inside Tamaki; the desire to return to America someday where she would have the opportunity to continue her education and improve her English. The two years at St. Mary passed very quickly for Tamaki and she was then faced with a decision regarding her future. She wanted to study in America and discussed this with her parents. At first they said no; not only because of the financial commitment, but because they thought America was a dangerous place to live in. However, Tamaki was persistent and her parents finally consented to her going abroad. Tamaki first entered the A.L.A. (American Language Academy) on the University of Portland campus arriving in early summer 1990. However, within a short period of time, she was able to score more than 500 points on the T.O.E.F.L. (Test of English as a Foreign Language) and was admitted into the University of Portland as a full time student in August, 1990. Soon to enter her second year of study in America, shared some of her experiences, thoughts, and feelings regarding life in America. When Tamaki entered an American University classroom, the first time she said it was a real shock. She couldn't believe how fast everyone talked. Even communicating and having basic conversations with American students was quite difficult in the beginning. She said, "Japanese students think they know English well, but when they get to America, they quickly find out that their English ability is limited and day to day life can be somewhat difficult in adjusting to college life in America. Tamaki said, the most difficult things for her were reading and lectures. She said that extensive reading homework assignments were made daily, while the lectures were very difficult to comprehend because all the teachers spoke very fast. At the same time, she was appreciative that the American teachers were very cooperative and gave her a lot of personal attention. She said that the teachers realize that Japanese students and other foreign students have some trouble in the beginning and are sensitive to this situation. In comparing the educational system of Japan to that of America, it is Tamaki's opinion that one must study harder in Japanese high schools, while just the opposite is true on the college level where one must study harder in American colleges and universities. When asked about social life, Tamaki commented that there were many sporting activities. She also said that dating was more popular in America and wherever you go, there are always couples together. She also feels that American young women are more mature for their age than Japanese women, and that the goals of American women are quite different from those of Japanese women. Most American female students that Tamaki has met are seeking professional careers where Japanese female students goals are usually to get an office job and to marry a few years later and raise a family. Tamaki feels that the difference in the two societies and cultures is the major reason for the difference in goals and personal development. She also commented on how much more independent American students are compared to Japanese. This is again based on the cultural differences between the two countries. Regarding day to day living, Tamaki finds life in America quite comfortable and enjoys living in a college dormitory. She is still amazed at how prices in America are so much lower than in Japan. However, when it comes to getting around or travelling, Tamaki misses the transportation convenience of Japan. She said that a person really needs to have an automobile to get anywhere. Tamaki also had some advice for Japanese students who hope to study abroad in the future, she said it is important for Japanese students to learn as much as possible about all aspects of Japan in order to respond to many types American students are quite inquisitive and want to know many things about Japan including culture, religion, politics, economics, etc. Tamaki felt that her knowledge in many of these areas was quite limited. Some other advice that Tamaki offers is to study English as hard as you can, be positive, be confident, set personal goals, and most of all, don't give up hope. In relating her own personal goals, Tamaki decided to study in America to improve her English speaking ability, to learn more about American culture, to gain personal independence, and to become more confident. She said her reasons were more personal development than aimed at career development.

Before she went to America, she said she was very dependent upon her parents for most everything. She also said she was a very shy person. But now, she has gained self confidence, she has become more mature and she has become quite independent. She said that most Japanese female students living abroad change in a similar manner. Tamaki Endo is very happy that she made the decision to go to America. Now, she's working in the business office as an interpreter and occasionally teaches English to the Japanese children. When asked the question, "What would you do differently if you had your life at St. Mary to do over again?" Tamaki immediately responded by saying, "I would have studied English harder.

ENGLISH CONVERSATION AS IDEOLOGY

I never heard the expression "English Conversation" (Eikaiwa) until I came to Japan. Of course the combination of words is understandable. But as it is used here, the expression "English Conversation" has the quality of slogan, in that it implies far more than speaking in the English language. The often heard sentence - "I want to learn how to speak English conversation" (rather than to 'speak English') is not redundant, as many English Teachers naively suppose. "English conversation" offers not simply Language training but a world view. Learning "English conversation" is not the same as learning how to speak English.

When I took my first English teaching job in Japan in 1990, I have taught "English conversation" from time to time in Language schools and company classes and I still find it embarrassing. I have struggled for a long time to try to understand just why the English conversation class is such an unsetting and alienating place. I once visited a conversation class at a major Tokyo Language school and found that it fitted the stereotype almost exactly. On the white wall was a poster of Disneyland. Five young women - all office workers - sat primly in a row and the teacher, an American woman, sat opposite them. They chanted in unison the following lesson:

A: Let's stop in this drug-store a minute.

B: Ok. I'd like to go in and look around. We don't have drugstores like this in Japan. We only sell a medicine.

A: Well, you can get medicine here, too. See that counter over there? That's the pharmacy department. The man who wears the white coat is the pharmacist.

B: Look at all the other things here - candy, newspapers, magazines, stationery, cosmetics. In Japan, we don't see such things at the drugstore.

A: Shall we go to the soda fountain?

B: What's the soda fountain?

A: Well, most drugstore have a soda fountain where you can get ice cream, soft drinks, sandwiches and so on.

B: Ok. Let's go!. I'm hungry. I'd like to get a hamburger and a milkshake.

As I watched these six human beings stare earnestly at each other across what seemed to be an impenetrable wall and repeat these sentences, the whole scene took an a surrealistic quality. How many hours, I wondered, have been spent in this country examining and re-examining the fabled American Drugstore and the legendary Real American Hamburger? It is embarrassing enough to have the impoverishment's of one's country's culture flaunted before people who have reason to know what true culture looks like, especially when there are so many other things in the world so much more worth talking about. But when one beings to suspect that perhaps the students are not repelled by the description of America's cultural wasteland, that perhaps, it is precisely these endless accounts of trips to the drugstore, the supermarket, the drive-in movie, and the hamburger stand that attract students to "English Conversation" schools, then the situation becomes truly humiliating.

Unfortunately, however, few English Teachers actually feel humiliated. While English teaching does not have the reputation among the foreign community here of being a especially rewarding work, it is considered to be relatively easy money. While there are a few teachers who try to do their job conscientiously, it is generally accepted this is not necessary. All that is really required is to be present in class and to talk about something or another. All the complex ethical problems are resolved by assuming an attitude of cultural superiority. The unspoken assumption of most of these teachers is that being in the presence of an English native speaker for an hour a week, is in itself a privilege worth paying for.

In the winter of 1990 when I had been in Japan as a presenter in ESL (English as a Second Language) in Arts and Crafts for JALT (The Japan Association of Language Teachers). Directions for the 90's, a friend told me that I could easily find a job teaching English. At that time I knew almost no Japanese, and so my acquaintances were almost entirely limited to people who could speak English. There was once an English Club in Tokyo where I was invited to attend and I was appalled at the obsequiousness which most of its members approached me I can remember listening incredulously as people told me that their "life's dream" was to become proficient at "English Conversation", that the place they would visit was Los Angeles. That their favorite novelist was Hawthorne, their favorite poet Longfellow, and so on. As far as I knew at the time, (and as far as the most foreigners who speak no Japanese know) these attitudes were representative of Japanese culture. It was only much later that I was able to discover that the world of "English Conversation" is only a subculture and not characteristic of Japanese University life.

I soon learned that the obsequious treatment which non-Japanese received from the English Club members was not to be understood as simply friendliness toward foreign guests. In the first place, it was not genuinely friendly: an attitude that treats one as a specimen rather than as a fellow human being is not the stuff out of which friendship can be built. But equally important, I soon learned that it was an attitude reserved only for a certain kind of foreigner. Later I moved to Nagoya City in central part of Japan and learned that the club was sponsoring a group of foreign students. I went to one meeting and found that the foreign students mostly from Southeast Asia were in a state of bitter anger. It seems that the club had sponsored a camping trip to foreign students, at which the member had followed the American and Europeans around like puppies (or like goldfish shit as you say in Japanese) while treating the Southeast Asians as if they were invisible. I shall never forget the expression on the club representative's face as he heard these angry complaints. It was clear that the club had never anticipated that its foreign students' members would be mostly filled with Asians. It was clear that they felt cheated, but were forced by the principles of "justice" to continue to sponsor the group. But obviously they wished nothing more than that these Southeast Asians would become invisible.

Another important lesson was taught me by a Japanese teacher at the English school where I was working. This old gentlemen came over to me one payday and told me gently, "There is something I think you should know. I have been working here for fifteen years, and you for three months, and yet my pay is less than yours. I am not criticizing, but I just think this is something you ought to know." He then left me alone to think it over by myself. I was shocked and confused. The man was a skilled linguist and an experienced teacher; I had been mostly getting through my class time by taking, telling jokes and stories that I thought up on the train on the way to work. Why should I get more money than he? Most of the people to whom I asked this question that it was because foreigners "need more dough to live on". But was this a real answer to the accusation of discrimination, or was it the essence of the discrimination itself?

To put the point as clearly as possible, the world of English conversation is racist. I do not wish to criticize the individual teachers and students of English, many of whom are serious and dedicated. I am talking about the ideology and structure of the subculture of "English Conversation". It is racist in its hiring practices, racist in its pay scale, racist in its advertising, and racist in ideology, put forward in its textbooks and classrooms.

For example, the idea of the "native speaker" is mostly a fraud. Especially the language schools that are run as business are proud of their "native speaker" and use them in their advertisements. But the expression "native speaker" is in effect a code word for "white". As I mentioned above, some of the "native speakers" come from European countries where English is not the native language. On the other hand, English is the official language in the Republic of the Philippines, Singapore, and in India, but people form those countries are not hired as native speakers. Occasionally they can find teaching jobs if they can prove their language ability, but on the whole they are rejected without examination. On the other hand, hiring is racist in that companies which specialized in hiring Americans tends to hire only white Americans. Of course in Japan the word "American" is for many people almost a synonym for "white", but as a matter of fact Americans come in all colors. Many Japanese Language schools fully weed out nonwhite candidates.

It is well known among the foreign community that for Caucasians who come to Japan with no job qualifications whatever, there are two kinds of work available. One is English teacher and the other is advertising model. A third possibility, for women who are willing to do it, is to become a stripper. The common point between these three forms of work is the fact that in Japan white skin itself can earn a profit. Every striptease house owner knows that the customers will pay more to see a "gaijin" (foreign) stripper if she can't dance. Every department store owner knows that he can't sell western clothing to women without a collection of blond, blue-eyed manikins that looks like a nazi dream of paradise. Every TV advertiser knows that he can increase sales simply by making a commercial showing Caucasians using the product. And every language schools knows that it can earn better profits with "native speakers" for English teachers.

(For contrast, ask yourself what kind of jobs are available in Japan for Filipinos, Koreans, Chinese, Thailanders, Indonesians and other Southeast Asians who come here with no job qualifications. Ask yourself if you have ever in your life seen a Caucasians employed in any of those in Japan.)

The preference for "native speakers" despite the lack of training and qualification is often defended from the standpoint of pronunciation. Southeast Asians, it is said, have bad pronunciation, and do American Blacks. It is the American Whites who speak "real" American English. But pronunciation is a relative thing. In both Britain and the United States of America there are many dialects and variation and within each country which of these is "standard" is a question decided by power: it is the language of the ruling class. Similarly, it is impossible to say that the variety of English that has been developed in the Republic of the Philippines is "incorrect". If the British could put together a new language out of Anglo-Saxon and French, and if the Americans could develop a new variety of that language in North America, then there is no reason why the Philippines cannot develop their own authentic variety of the language in Southeast Asia. The decision of which pronunciation you wish to study is not linguistic but political; it is a question of who you want to talk to.

I want to make clear that I think there are excellent reasons for studying English. It is the native language in a large number of countries and an important second language in many more. This is a fact that has a bloody history, it is the legacy of first the British, and then the American empires. Nevertheless, it is the case that English has become a language with which one can talk to people from almost any country in the world, a language which opens up new possibilities for international communication and solidarity and many levels.

I recognize that many Japanese people study English with the hope of being able to speak with other Asians, Africans and Europeans, but this hope is not reflected in the English conversation textbooks or classrooms. With the exception of the sector which emphasizes British English, in the world of "English conversation" the ideal speaking partner is always a White, middle class American. A glance through any of the textbooks will confirm this. In the boring little dramas that begin each lesson, at least one the protagonist is always American. Moreover the location of the stories is America if it not Japan. Money is always in dollars, measurement is always in yards, feet and inches, the drugstore always has a lunch counter and the groceries are always bought at a supermarket. If studying language is in any sense a kind of vicarious travel, if it is sometimes motivated by a desire to escape at least in imagination from the confines of one's own society, the English conversation texts channel and focus that desire on the U.S.A.

It is difficult for me to judge the depth of this identification of English conversation with the U.S.A. But I don't know that when a Caucasian of whatever nationality walks down a back street anywhere in Japan and encounters a group of little children playing, the first thing they will do is shout either "Ah, gaijin da", or "Ah Amerikajin da". The next thing they do, if they are old enough to have been to school, is to shout, "I have a book", "I have a pencil" and so on. This little scene, which rarely varies contains in primitive form several of the basic elements of the ideology of "English conversation". First of all (and to the endless annoyance of Europeans, Canadians, Latin Americans, Australians, etc.) to these children the words "gaijin" and "Amerikajin" are virtually synonyms. Not so much geographically as conceptually, "America" is the name for "that which is outside Japan;" it is "alternative" to Japanese culture. Moreover, it is built into the character of these "Amerigaijin" that they understand no Japanese, so that it is all right speak loudly about them while standing a few feet away ("Hana ga takai naa," etc.) If you want to respond to them in anyway, you use "Eng-" I have a pencil, etc. And the point is that you say these things whether or not you have a book or a pencil: it is a fundamental characteristic of "English conversation" that content is almost entirely irrelevant. But the odd thing about some saying "I have a book" to you when he has no book is that it is impossible to respond. Though the sentence is in English, it is not an attempt at communication. (Children uses to call out "haroo" which was real communication. Since then "I have a book" has become more common, presumably as a result of the advance of public education.) And in fact if one does say anything the children usually do not respond, but shout to each other "Eeeeeh, nihongo hanaseru," and sometimes run away in mock fear.

The adult world of English conversation is of course more sophisticated than what has mentioned in part there, but that only means that its ideology is more hidden. Of course all adults recognize that many countries exist, but often as little more than as stage props or background scenery (or sources of raw materials). When they are mentioned it is often out of fairness or to add a bit of cosmopolitan spice to the conversation. At a deeper level, cultural analysis takes the form comparison between the two real countries, Japan, and the United States of America. Put another way, in the world of "English Conversion," only Japan and the U.S. exist as categories, while all other countries exist as accidents. Of course there are many foreign countries, but the U.S. is foreigners itself, the historic alternative in comparison to which Japanese is defined, by imitation, contrast or some combination of the two.

To the great majority of Americans, this attitude seems only natural, since it fits quite nicely their own view of their country's position in the world. Among GIs in Asia, the slang expression for the U.S. in "the world". A letter from home is called a letter from the world, going back to the U.S. is called going back to the world, and so on. This is an extremely interesting expression, in that it exposes the American ideological self-image with rare precision. In this view, the world outside is simply not as real an the U.S. The very existence of that world is at a lower order of intensity: the events that take place there don't matter as much. This attitude is particularly strong in Asia, where to Americans everything seems upside down, contingent, unstable, accidental. Confronted with this confusing and apparently meaningless turmoil, the American takes comfort by conjuring up in his nostalgia the clean, ordered, and rational image of home. There is the corner drug store, for example, where almost anything you would want to buy is lined up neatly on the shelves. There is something you can understand, there is something real and sensible: there is The World itself.

Another way of putting this is that Americans see their own country as "universal" and all other countries especially in Asia and the Third World——as particular. Life in Japan is Japanese, life in the Philippines in Philippine, Life in Vietnam is Vietnamese, but life in the U.S. is life itself. It is not simply concrete living, it is also the idea of life, life which comes as close as this world allows to the principles of universal reason. Most Americans have deeply rooted belief that the way of life in their country is the way all people in the world choose to live if they had knowledge of it and the freedom to make the choice. In the 1950s, at the height of the cold war, it was seriously proposed in the U.S. that the Air Force should fly over Eastern Europeans saw all the wonderful things that Americans could buy. They would realize that they had been lied to by their soviet masters and rise up in revolt. The Peace Corps was in part based on a similar notion, namely that the mere appearance of a American youth in a traditional village would cause the local people to immediately start to throw off their old customs and try to learn to become like him. In American social science, this naïve and arrogant assumption appears again wearing the cloak of scientific objectively, and is called the demonstration effect. According to these American scholars, the turmoil in the Third World was not caused by colonialism and imperialism, but by what they call the revolution of rising expectations which was triggered by the mere exposure to aspects of modern life through demonstrations of machinery, buildings installations, consumer goods, show windows, rumors, governmental, medical, or military practices, as well as through mass media of communication. And of course the vanguard of so-called "modern life" is the United States of America.

This American attitude is particularly strong with regard to Japan because of the history of the Occupation. Even Americans who have nothing whatever about Japan have a vague historical memory of the Occupation. What they "remember" is that the Japanese didn't know how to run a modern, democratic country properly, and that the Americans sent Mac Arthur over to show them how.

As a consequence of these conditions, Americans tend to see the relation between the U.S.A. and Japan as that of teacher to student. This belief does not take the from of a conscious opinion but of an unconscious presupposition. That is, those who deny that their view will continue to act as if it is. At a very deep level Americans believe that they come from a society where things are rightly ordered, and consequently as soon as they step into Japanese territory. They are transformed from ordinary citizens into teachers. They are teachers not through any particular personal qualifications, but through their membership in a teacher culture. Thus it is perfectly natural to them that American drugstore, supermarket, drive-in restaurant, et...., since these are aspects of life in the living Utopia of which Japan is still only an imperfect, if earnestly striving, reflection. If the contempt implied in this set of attitudes of friendliness displayed by many Americans, remember that contempt is not necessarily an unfriendly attitude. One of the reasons why travel to Japan is so popular among Americans is that they can enjoy a sudden status boost and, usually for the first time in their liven, are treated as ruling class elites. "I love Japan," they say, "the service is so considerate."

The ideology of English conversation was born out of these American and Japanese attitudes. It is only in this context that the endless dwelling on the trivialities of American daily life in the textbook and classroom drills is comprehensible. Readers from whom it seems strange that a language lesson could contain an ideology might recall the famous sentence from the pre-war reader, "Susume, susume, heitai susume" (Advance, advance, soldier advance"). Propaganda in the form of language training has special subtlety; since attention is focused on the language lesson, the truth of the propaganda message is not discussed or questioned, but simply taken for granted. All those little conversation dramas which depict the American "way of life" as almost entirely composed of buying commodities at various stores are the very essence of the American propaganda. Or consider the following "substitution drill" which I copied out of a textbook:

He is intelligent but he has no drive.
He is intelligent but he has no money.
He is handsome but he has no money.
He is handsome but he has no girlfriend.
He is young but he has no girlfriend.
He is young but he has no ambition.

Intelligence, drive, money, good looks, girlfriends, youth ambition - a perfect profile of the condition of success for a man in capitalist in America. In effect the lesson reads, "Possess, possess, businessman possess."

To avoid misunderstanding, I should say that I think that the USA is a very interesting country and very well worth studying. The USA was an experimental country. It was a serious attempt to create in the New World a new kind of society which would provide the conditions for liberty, justice, equality and happiness that Europe had denied. The people who laid down the founding principles of this experiment were intelligent and learned, and this is all the more reason why the general failure of the society to provide the things promised should be a matter for a serious study.

But you will not be able to learn about this in the world of English conversation. The "America" that is depicted in that world is not the country that exist but the country that the American English teachers wish existed, the country of their nostalgia. In the world of English conversation, you will not learn why a spirit of disillusion and purposelessness pervaded that land today. You will not learn why the city streets are unsafe at night, why people carry weapons for self-protection, or why the most rapidly expanding department of government is the police. You will not learn why most American workers find their jobs deadening and senseless, why alcoholism and drug addiction is widespread among housewives, or why there are suburban areas in which the divorce rate is higher than the marriage. You will not learn why many Americans (mostly non-white) live in bitter and hopeless poverty, or why many of the children of the poor graduate from high school without having been taught to read. You will also not learn why, in American racist mentality, Japanese are categorized as colored, not as white.

Moreover, the problem is not simply that these facts about the US are not mentioned, but rather that the image of the country that is presented in the world of English conversation makes the truth more difficult to see.

It remains to describe how English conversation serves as a barrier to communication. Of course, people who have studied English conversation are very good at asking directions to the station and asking the price of purchases, but that is not the kind of communication I mean. Just how English conversation serves as a barrier is difficult to describe, but it is something that ones learn to sense before one begins to understand its specific content.

One year New Year's Eve, about five years ago, I was standing in a temple in Kanazawa listening to the great bell being rung at midnight. It had been snowing for several hours, the first snow of the winter, the new year had appeared in the form of the whole magnificent sound of the bell, a man came up to me and asked, "Excuse me, may I speak to you in English?" Complex thoughts filled my mind but I could only say, "Of course." Then he began to go through the standard list of questions:

Where are you from?
How long have you been in Japan?

Are you sightseeing in Kanazawa?
Can you eat Japanese food?
Do you understand what this ceremony is about?

His questions pushed me away from the mood of the ceremony, away from the sound of the bell and the smell of the cold air, away to the other side of the impenetrable wall of sakoku. His words were no more apt to the situation than, "I have a book." Nothing he said was really addressed to me, nor was he really interested in the answers. He was not speaking to me at all, but to the stereotype of the gaijin which he carried in his mind, of which my presence had only reminded him. Nor was it really he who was speaking to me. The sentences which he was reciting were in fixed and standard form, and it was difficult to believe that there was any relation between them and his own character, thoughts, or feelings. It was rather like a conversation between two tape recorders.

Finally, he moved away and another man, who had been watching my discomfort with some amusement, came over and said gently in Japanese, "Japanese who speak English like that don't know anything about Japan, so it's better not to pay them much attention." I felt tremendous gratitude, and started to laugh: the wall of sakoku had been broken down again.

Typically, "English conversation" is characterized by an attitude of obsequiousness, banality, a peculiar flatness or monotone, and practically no hint as to the identity or personality of the speaker. One Japanese friend who has done much study in the psychology of language, has suggested to me that at least in extreme cases, "English conversation" comes to take on an obsessional quality that resembles *aphasia*, an abnormal condition in which the subject's speech loses the capacity to deal with experience. My Japanese friend introduced me to a passage from **Paul Goodman**, in which he argues that...

...the obsessional man...who speaks with excruciating correctness, never modifying the common code to the situation or his purposes, is also aphasic. He does not speak the language but handles words... like concrete objects. All his sentences are stereotypes from the dictionary and the manual of grammar, if they fail him, or if he gets a lively response, or if his impulsive needs are too strong for this rigid use of language, he will break down.

Interesting, it is often the most diligent "English conversation" students who fit this description most closely. Though only a few people reach this extreme degree of alienated speech, most undergo a radical personality change - perhaps better described as a personality loss - when speaking "English conversation."

It seems to be assumed that the Japanese of expressing spirit, wit, anger, respect, affection and beauty of form cannot be communicated in the English language. The texts demand that the students take on an ill-fitting "American" personality and relate to each other in unfamiliar was. But of course, this textbook personality expresses no human character; it is a caricature of American white middle class personality, and is capable of only a kind of vague and stilted casualness. This vague casualness expresses neither the intimacy due friends and family nor the respect due others. Adoption of this empty personality is an offense to dignify. This is one of the most important obstacles in English study: it causes many people to stay away from "English conversation" altogether for reasons of pride. Obviously, it is not a difficulty that can be overcome by strictly linguistic training.

This problem is not simply by the fact that Japan is an island country whose people are not accustomed to dealing with foreigners. The characteristics I am talking about are a consequence of the ideology of English conversation. The English spoken by people who learned it outside the subculture of eikaiwa - for example, people who studied it before the war, people who immigrated to the US, working class people who picked it up on their jobs at U.S. bases or at other places where English is used - has quite different characteristics. Moreover, people who have recognized the ideology, consciously rejected it, and studied the language on a different basis also speak a much more natural and communicative form of English. The farther away one gets from the world of "English conversation" the weaker cultural barriers become. Whenever I have traveled in the countryside, for example the place were foreigners are the most rarely seen, I have found that the people there were far more natural, open, and dignified in their attitude toward me than are people in the world of "English conversation." There, I have always been treated as an equal, and since the people could observe that I was a human being, they were astounded by anything I did - for example eat Japanese or speak in Japanese. The same is generally true among working class people. Among intellectuals and middle class people, the most natural attitude is, as I have mentioned, found among people who have stayed attitude is, as far away as they could from the world of "English conversation."

I can understand that the world of "English conversation" might serve as useful function. I can see how the Japanese people might instinctively develop a wall of callus around their culture, to protect its more delicate areas from the bruising attacks of Western harshness and aggressiveness. But I wonder if many readers realize that for most English-speaking visitors, the world of "English conversation" is almost the only Japan they encounter. They live almost entirely in the subculture that speaks English without realizing that it is a subculture, without understanding that the culture, personality characteristics and attitudes that they take to be those of Japan are in reality those of the ideology of "English conversation." It's something to think about.

But mean this to be an appeal to improve communication with Western visitors. How they are treated is not important. What is important is to destroy the ideology of "English conversation", to stop thinking of it as the language of Asian and the Third World solidarity. When English study is transformed from a form of toadying into a tool of liberation, all the famous special difficulties which the Japanese are supposed to have with English will probably vanish like the mist. Language schools which employ only Caucasian teachers should be boycotted. Japanese who want to study English should form study groups with Southeast Asians, and together work out a new Asian version of English that reflects the style, culture, history, and politics of Asia. And then, if the Americans who come to Asia complain that they can't understand this new variety of English, they should be sent to language school.

A PROGRAM OF ARTS AND CRAFTS IN JAPAN

A curriculum of Arts studies is desired in the organization of any school program. arts has its own body of knowledge, principles and elements which provide the framework for the other functions it has. The Art educators role is to stimulate the individuals basic need for creative activity, a need which is not restricted to the select few who are talented. It is important of Art in the students an aesthetic awareness based on the elements of art and to realize how this awareness is applied to everyday living. The Art educator facilitates the development of self-expression, self-esteem, problem solving, observation skills, etc. for the students through guided study.

This program also offers the students the opportunity to develop their interest, talents, skills and dexterity. As a consequence of concrete achievements, students increase self-confidence and prepare them for adaptation into another culture.

Arts and Crafts as a subject serves as a tool for non-verbal outlet for expressing students creativity. It can develop their talent creative abilities and widen the sphere of their artistic imagination.

Suggested lessons and activity will provide the students the opportunity to observe experiment and to participate in creative activities and to explore other culture thru Arts. To facilitate understanding and participation, vocabulary words related to the specified Art area shall be introduced and unlocked.

1. Printmaking:

Students will learn how to make print designs either for decorative purposes like using plant stalks and how to print T-shirt by using textile paints. This is offered to motivate students to make use of their art skills profitably since silk screen, printed T-shirt are in demand in the market today. Wearing one is a fad and a "craze" among teenagers and old alike.

2. Weaving:

Knowledge of this art area will test the students' imaginative skills by using string in art work. In this, they will employ angles to form designs and discover the effects line intersections. This will help improve students decision making capability in doing the process.

3. Pottery:

The students will find out that pottery making is an excellent means of self-expression. With it they can experiment on new and exciting shapes. They could start with the simplest method of pottery-making coil method. This method was already used by the early American Indians who were found to be very skillful in the art.

Other Dimensional Arts and Crafts

This subject will teach the students to create thru paper crafts and identify various shapes to express ideas. These activities include the following:

1. Origami
2. Collage
3. Paper Mache
4. Paper Masks
5. Paper Tapestry
6. Paper Tearing

For much of its history, art has been an educational extra, a valuable subject but not an essential. We believe it belongs at the core!! We believe it should be in the mainstream of every educational level. Why? Because Art means three things that everyone wants and need.

Arts Means Work

Over and above creativity, self-expression and communication art is a type of work. This is what Art has been from the beginning. This is what Art is from childhood to old age. Through Art, our students learn the meaning and joy of work, work done to be best of one's ability, for its own sake, for the satisfaction of a job well done. There is a desperate need in our society for a revival of the idea of good work. Work for personal fulfillment; work for social recognition; work for economic development. Work is one of the noblest expressions of the human spirit, and art is the visible evidence of work carried to the highest possible level. Today we hear much about productivity and workmanship. Both of two concepts have their roots in art. We are dedicated to the idea that art is the best way for every young person to learn the value of work.

Art Means Language

Art is a language of visual images and expression that everyone uses. In art classes we make visual images and we study visual images. Increasingly, these images affect our needs, our daily behavior, our hopes, our opinions and our ultimate ideals that is why the individual who cannot understand or read images is incompletely educated. Complete literacy includes the ability to understand, respond to, and talk to create about visual images. Therefore, to carry out its total mission, Art education stimulates language-spoken and written-about visual images. As Art Teachers we work continuously on the development of critical skills. This is our way of encouraging linguistic skills.

By teaching our students to describe, analyze and interpret visual images, we enhance their powers of verbal expression that has no education frill.

Art Means Value

You cannot touch Art without touching values. Values about home and family, work and play the individual and society, nature and the environment, war and peace, beauty and ugliness, violence and love. The great art of the past and the present deals with these durable human concerns. Through history we learn about people through their art. As Art teachers we do not indoctrinate. But when we study the art of many lands and people we expose our students to the expression of a wide range of human values and concerns. We sensitize students to the fact that values exist and that visual images reflect their value choices. All of them should be given the opportunity to see how Art expresses the highest aspirations of the human spirit.

Art thrives when its skills and imagination are attached to authentic personal concerns, genuine human problems, real, social needs!!!

Nevertheless, I believe the well-prepared art teacher does a good job on the "Art means language" statement. And most of us trying hard to perform on the "Art means Values" statement. The effort alone deserves support. It is really important not only for our professional survival but also for the sake of our students, for the schools, and for our society.

It's all well and good to try to influence decision-maker to protest the cut-back of Art positions, and to insist that art instruction deserves more support from school boards, curriculum developers, guidance counselors, and the like. But it is more important to inform these people about the concrete things does Art to advance their educational objectives. Thus, Creating Art involves internal struggle, making choices, solving problems, expressing one's self.

ENGLISH IN ARTS AND CRAFTS

Arts and Crafts as a means of total self-expression is utilized by sharing common experience, exchange of ideas and techniques, thus **Feedbacking** is attained by comparing tangible results based on individual output leading to the development of better communication.

TRADITIONAL TOYS IN JAPAN

The Japanese archipelago lies along, narrow are just off the Asian continent, running northeast to southwest from the subarctic zone all the way to the tropics. Each region of the country boasts an assortment of distinctive dolls and toys reflecting the richness of local cultures.

Toys created and developed in a particular locality began to proliferate during the Edo period (1603 - 1867), during which Japan enjoyed a long peace under the Tokugawa shogunate. Tokugawa Japan was divided into semi-autonomous fiefdoms ruled by some 270 feudal lords or daimyos. Often, these fiefdoms were in valleys, with the towns centered around the daimyo's castle. The isolated communities were self-contained and self-supporting. In time, as a commercial economy grew and regions began to interact more, creative local cultures evolved. Children's playthings, lovingly crafted, were one expression of each region's genius.

In castle towns, for example, in between crafting tiles for the daimyo's castle or a samurai's home, a tile maker might pause to make clay dolls for the neighborhood children. Or a shopkeeper, finished with an account book made of *washi* (Japanese paper), would glue the sheets together, fashion them into different shapes, such as animals, and paint them in bright colors to make a *hariko*, a papier-mache toy. Women would gather scraps of cloth and thread to make colorful balls, or bits of colored wrapping paper to make fancy paper dolls.

In remote agricultural areas, people fashioned the dried husks of rice and barley, their staple foods, into horses, offering to the gods in prayer for a bountiful harvest. Reed pipes, tops, windmills, bamboo pea-shooters, dolls, and toy horses were contrived out of other plants. Mountain dwelling communities produced simple, cylindrical wooden dolls known as *kokeshi*. In this way, each region produced folk toys imbued with local flavor.

From about the mid-18th century, sophisticated toys from big cities, such as Edo (present-day Tokyo), Osaka and Kyoto, were introduced by the daimyos to outlying regions. These toys had a profound impact on a traditional folk craft: Regional craftspeople imitated urban styles but without sacrificing local individuality, and the dolls and toys they crafted became works of industrial art. Handmade objects that had once been fashioned sporadically in homes gradually developed into manufactured commercial products.

Clay dolls made in Fushimi, Kyoto, are the oldest such dolls in Japan, dating back to the early 17th century when they were sold as mascot trinkets near Fushimi Inari Shrine. By the late 19th century, over 100 localities nationwide sold similar clay dolls; they had become an indispensable part of Hina Matsuri, the girls' doll festival. Every March, when the festival was celebrated, doll fairs would be held around the country so that loving parents might buy a set of dolls for their daughter to display at home, amid hopes for the girl's good health and future happiness in marriage.

Dolls were also bought and sold on crowded fair days at local shrines or temples. Dolls and other toys became salable commodities by virtue of their association with seasonal events such as Hina Matsuri, but they were also widely popular as talismanic keepsakes, or *omiyage* (souvenirs), bought to gain divine protection.

According to ethnologists, *omiyage* originally meant "something given by a deity." It derives from *miya* (shrine) and *ge* (sacred vessel). Crowds of the faithful would go to shrines or temples to pray to Shinto or Buddhist deities and then purchase dolls as souvenirs.

Many old toys and dolls are conspicuously red. The color red was believed to have the power to cure such children's diseases as the measles. Old playthings that convey the timeless depth of parents' concern for their children are filled with a simple, warm beauty.

The many traditional handmade toys that developed in Tokugawa Japan were made of simple, readily available natural materials. After the Meiji Restoration of 1868, however, Japan entered a new era in which toys, like everything else, were profoundly affected. The long period of national isolation came to an end, and Japan was introduced to modern toys imported from the advanced nations of the West.

Admired as *hakuraihin* - high - quality goods imported by ship - modern toys were eagerly sought after by children all over Japan. The old-fashioned folk craft toys quickly fell out of favor. Once-loved playthings that had passed from generation to generation faded from the scene, seemingly forgotten. But some 20 years after the country was opened, in reaction to the enthusiastic welcome given to all aspects of American and European culture, people began to feel stirrings of nostalgia for the old Japanese ways.

In 1891, a large collection of drawings was published that a portrayed folk dolls and toys from around the country. Group of enthusiasts began collecting samples of old toys. In this way, the traditional folk craft items that children, swept up in the trend toward modernization, had turned their backs on were rescued from oblivion and given new vitality through the efforts of a few dedicated adults. Today, a century later the passion of these men and women lives in many others.

The rustic toys of provincial Japan - especially the dolls - also approved popular among non-Japanese. In 1890, Lafcadio Hearn (1850-1904) an American newspaperman, came to teach English in Matsue, a castle town in Western Japan. There, he became attracted to the distinctive beauty of local *anesama ningyo* (big sister dolls). He described them at length in his book Glimpses of Unfamiliar Japan (1894) and sent samples to the British Museum in London.

In the 1920s, the American anthropologist Frederick Stael, a frequent visitor to Japan, touched on Hern's observations in his own writings. Nothing that dolls and toys similar to those Hearn had written of some 30 years earlier were still being made in his own day, Stael questioned why they had survived. He concluded that the methods of production might be simple and rough, he said, and the form and conception of the toys naïve, but their colors were extraordinary vivid - overall, they bore great testimony to the artistic and emotional character of the men and women who created them.

Felipe CoFreros, Ph.D.

At present, some 3,000 varieties of provincial toys are produced nationwide. A dozen special museums display collections of once-common toys numbering in the tens of thousands. Traditional folk toys survive in especially large numbers in northeastern Japan, home of many of the works pictured in the preceding pages.

THE PACHINKO GAME IN JAPAN

PACHINKO is primarily a game, one calling for "a combination for strategy, skill and luck." Although the aim is simply "to get more balls out of the machine than you put into it," there is more to pachinko than that. Pachinko is Japan's true national sport. One-fourth of the population, about 30 million Japanese plays the game occasionally or habitually. To do so, they spend more money than does the nation on national on national defense. It is estimated that the legitimate pachinko take is between 5 trillion to 10 trillion yen per year. Some say the figure is understated by at least 20 percent. Whatever, pachinko is also said to be the largest single industrial tax evader in Japan.

Nonetheless, its success is complete and growing. There are now over 16,000 pachinko parlors in the country, and they are stocked, it is said, with 4 million machines. The pachinko game is truly popular. To any outsider wandering in, the question must be; Why? For what reason would these masses sit immobile, apparently mesmerized, in front of their clattering machine, enduring the noise, the ubiquitous tobacco smoke, the uniform fluorescent glare and the merciless iterations of the "Gunkan March."

Pachinko is also Japan's favorite form of gambling and during its long history the national Police agency has its attention constantly called to it. Originally, it was a child's game, called korinto gemu, a copy of an early American pinball apparatus called Corinthian game, imported from Chicago by an Osaka firm around 1924. In true native fashion it was shortly improve out of all recognition, one of the enhancements being a way to utilize the gambling potential.

Pachinko came into its own as a gambling device only after the war in Nagoya City, Japan in 1946. In the lean and gray postwar years, the game was not only a way to pass the time but also, says Eric Sedensky, the author of the game of Japanese Pinball; a way to make money. And this potential has continued and expanded. The pachinko pro according to the author, spends between 20,000 and 100,000 yen a day and can take home anywhere between 40,000 and 150,000 yen. A good pro can make up half a million a month, this he does in a number of ways: finding the right machine, testing out its possibilities, settling in for long term-term strategy, getting just the right amount of skill in the turn of the ball-propelling knob.

The reason for all this preparation and precaution is that the machine, like life itself, changes overnight. A person call a kugishi comes in and realigns the pins through which the ball fall. Hired by the establishment, he makes certain that yesterday's machine is no longer worth the trouble. His is a delicate task. He must keep the pins wide

AN ASIAN BRIDE FOR THE JAPANESE

Lonely farmers in Japan's rugged remote regions who look overseas for a bride are now receiving some official help - as are the women who marry for money but struggle to settle in a land of alien customs and language.

Since the mid-1980s, women from South Korea, the Philippines, China and elsewhere in Asia have been taking the place of thousands of Japanese who fled harsh country life for job opportunities in the cities.

Commercial brokers arranged marriages. Some prospered, others ended in divorce, lawsuits or suicide.

A recent nationwide conference on the marital plight of the farmers decided that overseas brides would continue arriving.

Local governments now offer farmers introduction services to potential brides, both Japanese and foreign. Local authorities and volunteer groups teach brides Japanese and advise and support them after wedding.

The government publishes no statistics but estimates put the number of such wives across Japan at several thousand.

Most are married to farmers in remote areas of the north and west, which have suffered the worst from depopulation.

City official Eimitsu Kazama, from Tokamachi, Niigata Prefecture, said there was no sign that more Japanese women were prepared to stay down on the farm. So the influx of Asian brides looked set not just to continue but to increase.

"If we want to maintain continuity of life in these areas, it is necessary," he said. Takeshi Takeda, an official of the National Farmer's Cooperative from Yamagata Prefecture, agreed the shortage of Japanese wives would continue.

"Most of the international marriages are successful but the newspapers report only one side. Most couples have a good life together," Takeda said.

There are about 250 Asian brides in Yamagata, a mountainous region with a long, harsh winter that depends mainly on growing rice and fruit and on forestry.

Dr. Norihiko Kuwayama set up a center for the 88 Asian and other foreign brides in his district, Mogami-gun, to offer both medical and psychological help.

Fifty are from South Korea, 33 from the Philippines and the others from China, Brazil and Honduras.

"The most important point is that they cannot speak any Japanese, and the Japanese family knows nothing of the culture and customs of their countries," he said.

Kuwayama carries a portable telephone that the women can call at any time.

He said December to February was the most difficult time, when the weather was bleakest and many husbands went away for months to work in Tokyo.

Christian brides were unable to celebrate Christmas as they used to.

A farmer pays Y3 million to Y4 million for a Korean bride, some of which goes to her family. The cost of a Philippine bride in the late 1980s was about half that, with part going to her family.

Couples usually meet for no more a week before the marriage.

The woman, who often feels obliged to support her family in her impoverished homeland, wants to make money. The man wants companionship and sometimes a son to inherit the ancestral land and preserve village life.

The unions have mixed results. In the village of Okura in Yamagata, 12 Japanese men have married Filipinos since 1987.

One marriage counselor from Niigata said that, despite many problems, the 17 Asian brides in her district were adjusting well and had been accepted by the local community.

She said they were enthusiastically studying Japanese and those who wished could attend church and send money they earned themselves back to their family.

"They feel more fortunate than if they had stayed at home," she said.

Brides also faced problems over family relationships.

Kuwayama said a typical case was an introvert husband unable to express himself freely or to stand up to his bride's all-powerful mother-in-law.

Marriage has seldom been easy in Japan's poorer rural areas.

Before the postwar economic miracle, many families could not support their daughters and sent them to work in the cities as laborers, maids or prostitutes.

The eldest son could find a wife because he would inherit his father's land. Younger brothers often had to stay bachelors.

BIBLIOGRAPHY

Abel, Theodora M. Psychological Testing in Cultural Contexts. New Haven: College and University Press, 1973.

Abridged from the New York Teachers of English to Speakers of other Languages and Bilingual Association guidelines

Adams, Parveen, editor: Language and Thinking. New York: Penguin books, 1972.

Aquino, Gaudencio V. Principles and Methods of Effective Teaching, National Bookstore Inc., Manila, Philippines, 1988

Bassano, Consonants Sound Easy

Berry and Dasen. Culture and Cognition: Readings in Cross-Cultural Psychology, London; Methuen and Co., 1974.

Blanton, Linda Lonon. Elementary Composition Practice, Books I and II (Rowley Mass: Newbury House) 1978 and 1979.

Blanton, Linda Lonon. Intermediate Composition Practice. Book I Sequel to Elementary Composition Practice.

Bodman, Jean and Michael Lanzao. No Hot Water Tonight (New York: Collier Macmillan International, Inc.) 1975.

Bodman, Jean and Michael Lanzao. No Cold Water Either Sequel to No Hot Water Tonight.

Boyd, John R. and Mary Ann Boyd. Alice Blows a Fuse: Fifty Strip Stories in American English (Englewood Cliffs, N.J.: Prentice - Hall, Inc.) 1980.

Branouw, Victor. Culture and Personality, Illonois: The Dorsey Press, 1963.

Brislin, Bochner Lonner. Cross-Cultural Perspective on Learning. New York: Halstead Press Division, John Wiley and Sons, Sage Publications, 1975.

Brookes, Gay and Jean Withrow. 10 Steps: A Course in Controlled Composition for Beginning and Intermediate ESL Students. (New York: Language Innovations, Inc.) 1974.

Bryson, Bill. The Mother Tongue, New York: William Morrow, 1990.

Bruner, Edward. The Concept of Experience. "Experience and Expressions"

Carell, John B., editor. Language, Thought and Reality. (Writings of B.L. Whorf)

Clovis Adult School, Life School (Belmont, CA: Pitman Learning, Inc.) 1981.

CoFreros, Felipe A., Ph.D., Author. Effective Ways To Assess English Language Learners: Xlibris Publishing Company, USA 2012

CoFreros, Felipe A., Ph.D., Author. A Handbook of Writing Activities For Intermediate and Advanced English Language Learners - Xlibris Publishing Company, U.S.A. 2015

Deutsch, M. Cooperation and Trust. An M. Jones (ed.) Nebraska Symposium on Motivation. Lincoln, NE: Univ. of Nebraska Press, 1962

"Educational Development Through Research and Evaluation", A write-up provided by the Southeast Asian Ministers of Education organization Regional Center for Educational Innovation and Technology, July 4, 1988.

Evangelista, Rafael, "Education in the New Government - What it should be: A voice of a Parent," Education and Culture Journal, Volume 3 No. 2, Oct.-Dec., 1996

Finocchiaro, Mary and Violet Hoch Lavenda. Selections for Developing English Language Skills (New York: Regents) 1973.

Fuglesang, Andreas, Applied Communication in Developing Countries, Ideas and Observations, The Dag Hammarskjold Foundation, 1973

Graham, Jazz Chants

Gregorio, Herman. Principles and Practices of College Teaching, R.P. Garcia Publishing Inc., Quezon City, Philippines, 1977.

Guidelines for the Tutor in teaching English as a Second Language. (Los Angeles: Los Angeles City Schools, 1970), p. 125 Japan Quarterly, Jan.-Mar., 1990.

Haverson, Wayne W. and Judith L. Haynes. Modulearn ESL Literacy Program (San Juan Capistrano, CA: Modulearn, Inc.) 1980.

Heaton, J.B. Composition Through Pictures (London: Longman) 1966.

Heaton J.B. Beginning Composition Through Pictures (London: Longman) 1975.

Hecht and Ryan, Survival Pronunciation

Honigmann, John, Personality in Culture. New York: Harper and Row, 1967.

Hotta, A. and Ishiguro, Y. (1986). A guide to Japanese Hot Springs. New York: Kodansha International, Ltd.

Howell, Richard W. Language in Behavior, New York: Human Sciences Press, Behavioral Publications, 1976.

Kondo, Dorine, Krafting Selves: Power, Gender and Discourses of Identity in a Japanese Workplace. Chicago: University of Chicago Press, 1990.

Kubota, Mayumi. Implications of Back Channel Behavior in Japanese and English Conversation. 1991

Kunz, Linda Ann. 26 Steps: A Course in Controlled Composition for Intermediate and Advanced Students (New York: Language Innovations, Inc.) 1973.

Landar, Herbert. Language and Culture. Oxford: Oxford University Press, 1966.

Lardizabal, Amparo. Principles and Methods of Teaching, Phoenix Publishing House, Inc., 1977.

Levin, Beatrice Jackson. Real Life Writing Skills (New York: Scholastic Book Services) 1979.

Longfield, Diane M. Passage to ESL Literacy (Arlington Heights, III: Delta Systems, Inc.) 1981.

Lyons, V. (ed.) Structuring Cooperative Learning in the Classroom: The 1980 Handbook. Minneapolis, MN: Interaction Books, 1980.

Markley, Rayner W. Handwriting Workbook: Handwriting and Letter Recognition Practice for Learners of the English Alphabet (USA: English Language Services) 1977.

Mc Harris, R. and Beeson, G. W., "Writing the Research Proposal" in G.W. Beeson Edition, Research in Education, Roden State College, (Melbourne, Australia, 1981) p. 164

Morley, Listening Dictation

Nakane, Chic. "Japanese Society" (Weidenfeld and Nicolson, 1970)

Ochs, Elinor. Culture and Language Development, Cambridge: Cambridge University Press, 1988.

Paulston, Christina Bratt and Gerald Dykstra. Controlled Composition in English as a Second Language (New York: Regents) 1973.

Raimes, Anna. Focus on Composition (New York: Oxford University Press) 1978.

Realize Magazine, Volume 2 Spring 1994, Nagoya, Japan

Refugee Digest/ Newsletter Volume I No. 2 and 3 First Quarter 1990. International Catholic Migration Commission (ICMC), Southeast Asia Refugee Camp

Rheingold, Howard. They have a word for it. Los Angeles: Jeremy P. Tarcher, Inc., 1988

Rivera, Filomena V. and Sembrano, Guillerma, Towards Effective Teaching, National Bookstore, Manila, Philippines, 1980.

Rivers, Wilga Teaching Foreign Language Skills: Chicago, University of Chicago Press, 1968

Robinson, Lois Guided Writing and Free Writing (New York: Harper and Row) 1967.

Roland, Allan. In Search of Self in India and Japan. Princeton: Princeton University Press, 1988.

Rost and Straton, "Pronunciation Exercises" in Listening Transition

Roy, P. (ed.) Structuring Cooperative Learning in the Classroom: The 1982 Handbook. Minneapolis, MN: Interaction Books, 1982.

Sapir, Edward. Language, Culture and Personality. Ann Arbor: "O - P Book" University Microfilm, Inc., 1962

Segall, Campbell and Herskovits. The influence of culture on visual perception. New York: Bobs - Mcrill Co., 1966

Segall, Marshall H. Cross - Cultural Psychology: Human behavior in Global Perspective. New York: Brooks / Cole Publishing, 1979.

Shweder and Le Vine. Culture Theory, Cambridge University Press, 1984

Vockell, Edward L. Educational Research. (New York: Mcmillan Book Co., Inc., 1983), p. 254

Wordell, Charles B., A Guide to teaching English in Japan, The Japan Times, Ltd., 1985.

GLOSSARY

absurdity	n.	The quality of being absurd
accelerate	vb.	To cause to act or move faster; increase the speed of
acquisition	n.	The act of acquiring; anything gained or won; a power or possession
affiliation	n.	1. The act of affiliating, or the state of being affiliated; association; friendly relationship; connection; adoption 2. combination; union
affliction	n.	1. The state of being afflicted; sore distress of body or mind 2. That which causes great suffering or distress; misfortune; calamity
aggression	n.	1. An unprovoked attack; encroachment 2. Habitual aggressive action or practices

alienate	vb.	1. To make indifferent or unfriendly; estrange 2. To cause to feel estrange or withdrawn from society 3. To make over; transfer, as property to the ownership of author 4. To turn away, as affection or interest
anecdotal	adj.	Pertaining to, characterized by, or consisting of anecdotes
annoyance	n.	1. An annoying or being annoyed 2. One who or that which annoys
aphasia	n.	1. Partial or total loss of the ability to articulate or understand language due to damage to the cerebral cortex 2. An abnormal condition in which the subjects speech loses the capacity to deal with experience
appal	vb.	To fill with dismay or horror; terrify; shock
arsenal	n.	A public repository or manufactory of arms and ammunitions of war.
Asahi Shimbun	n.	A popular newspaper publication in Japan.
asylum	n.	A place of refuge; retreat; shelter
auditory	adj.	Of or pertaining to hearing or the organs or sense of hearing.
	n.	An assembly of hearers; an audience.
automatons	n.	1. A contrivance or apparatus that appears to function of itself by the action of the concealed mechanism. 2. Any living being whose actions are or appear to be involuntary or mechanical. 3. Anything capable of spontaneous movement or action.

badge	n.	1. A token, mark, decoration, or insigma of office, rank or membership 2. Any distinguishing mark
banal	adj.	Lacking originality, freshness or novelty
bedridden	adj.	Confined to bed, by sickness or weakness
bilingual	adj.	1. Recorded or expressed in two languages 2. Speaking two languages
bloc	n.	A group, as of politicians, combined to foster special interests or to obstruct legislative action.
Bo	n.	A Japanese word for mother.
bootstrap	n.	A loop strap sewed at the side or the rear top of a boot to help in pulling it on.
	adj.	Designed to function independently of outside direction
	vb.	To promote or to develop by individual initiative and effort with a minimum of outside assistance
borough	n.	An incorporated village or town; a subdivision of a city, having a limited self-government
brevity	n.	1. Shortness of duration; brief time 2. Condensation of language; conciseness
cajun	n.	A reputed descendant of the Acadian French in Louisiana
callus	n.	A callosity of thickening
caricature	n.	A picture of description deliberately making use of ridiculous exaggeration or distortion.

Caucasians	n.	1. A member of the white-skinned division of the human race; so called found in the Caucasus, which was taken as establishing the type 2. A member of the native peoples of the Caucasus region
caution	n.	1. Care to avoid injury or misfortune; prudence; wariness 2. An admonition of warning
cheery	adj.	Marked by cheerfulness or good spirits
cloak	n.	1. A loose outer garment 2. Something that covers or hides; a pretext; a disguise; mask
colonialism	n.	The policy of nation seeking to acquire, extend or retain overseas dependencies; imperialism
compel	vb.	1. To drive or urge irresistibility; constrain 2. To force to yield; subdue 3. To obtain by force; exact
comprehension	n.	The mental grasping of ideas, facts, etc., or the power of doing so.
connotation	n.	The suggestive emotional content or significance of a word, additional to its explicit literal meaning; implication
consensus	n.	A collective opinion; general agreement
contemporary	adj.	1. Contemporaneous; living or existing at the same time 2. Having the same age; coeval
contingent	adj.	1. Likely to occur 2. Pertaining to contraception
	n.	Any device or substance that inhibits conception

contradictory	adj.	1. Involving or of the nature of a contradiction; inconsistent; contrary 2. Given or inclined to contradiction
cosmopolitan	adj.	1. Common to all the world; not local or limited 2. At home in all parts of the world
defy	vb.	1. To resist or disregard openly or boldly 2. To challenge 3. To resist successfully; baffle; obstruct
dexterity	n.	1. Readiness and skill in using the hands; expertness 2. Mental quickness, adroitness or skill
diagnostician	n.	One who is versed in diagnosis
dichotomy	n.	The state of being divided in two; division into two pairs
dilemma	n.	A necessary choice between equally undesirable alternatives, a perplexing predicament
discrimination	n.	1. The act of power of discriminating; the discernment of distinctions 2. Differential treatment; bias 3. The state or condition of being discriminated; distinction
distort	vb.	1. To twist or bend out of shape; make crooked or mishappen 2. To twist the meaning of; misrepresent; pervert
doom	vb.	1. To pronounce judgment or sentence upon; condemn 2. To destine to a disastrous fate
	n.	1. The act of dooming, or the state of being doomed 2. Death; ruin; sad or evil destiny

dough	n.	1. A soft mass of moistened flour or meal, mixed for cooking into bread, cake, etc. 2. Any soft pasty mass 3. <u>Slang</u> - money
dubious	adj.	1. Unsettled in judgment or opinion; in a state of doubt; doubtful 2. Being a subject matter of doubt; causing doubt 3. Of uncertain result; not yet settled; problematic 4. Being the occasion of doubt; difficult of explanation; equivocal
earnest	adj.	1. Intent and direct in purpose; zealous; fervent of persons 2. Marked by deep feeling of conviction; heart-felt; hearty: of words or acts
eccentricity	n.	1. The state or quality of being eccentric; oddity 2. An odd or capricious act 3. The distance between the centers of two eccentric circles or objects 4. The condition or quality of being eccentric
efficacy	n.	Power to produce an effect; effective energy
eikaiwa	n.	English conversation
elicit	vb.	To draw out or forth, as by some attraction or inducement; bring to light
encroachment	n.	1. Entrance upon the rights or domain of another; especially, gradual intrusion
endeavor	n.	An attempt or effort to do or attain something; earnest exertion for an end
	vb.	To make an effort to do or effect; try; usually with an infinitive as object

ersatz	n.	A substitute; equivalent; replacement, usually inferior to the original product or material
ethnocentrism	n.	The concept, formulated by W. G. Sumner, that the attitudes, beliefs, and customs of one's own group, nation, or people are of central importance and of a basis for judging all other groups
exacerbate	vb.	To make more violent, bitter, or severe
excruciating	adj.	Causing or inflicting intense pain; agonizing
	vb.	To inflict extreme pain or agony upon; torture
exorbitant	adj.	1. Not coming within the scope of the law 2. Exceeding in intensity, quality, amount or size the customary or appropriate limits
extriction	n.	Cessation of a particular behavior
fatalistic	adj.	Believing in fatalism
fixture	n.	1. Anything fixed firmly in its place 2. One who or that which is regarded as permanently fixed
flaky	n.	Resembling or consisting of flakes; easily separable into flakes
flaunt	vb.	1. To make an ostentatious or gaudy display; parade impudently 2. To wave or flutter freely 3. To show or display in an ostentatious or impudent manner
	n.	1. The act of flaunting 2. A boast; vaunt
foreigner	n.	"gaijin" in Japanese A native or citizen of a foreign country

fraud	n.	Deception in order to gain by another's loss; craft; trickery guile
frenzied	adj.	Affected with frenzy or madness, frantic
frill	n.	An ornamental band of textile fabric, especially of lace or fine lawn, gathered in folds on one edge, the other edge being left loose; a flounce; ruffle
frugal	adj.	1. Exercising economy; saving; sparing 2. Marked by economy; meager; stinted
gaijin	adj.	Foreigner
gait	n.	1. One's manner of moving along on foot. 2. One of the ways in which a horse steps or runs.
gobbledygook	adj.	A 1940's term for bloated, empty words
indoctrinate	vb.	1. To instruct especially esp. in fundamentals or rudiments; teach 2. To imbue with a usu. Partisan or secretarian opinion, point of view or principle.
inference	n.	The act of inferring; a deduction or conclusion
influx	n.	A coming in
innate	adj.	1. Existing in, belonging to, or determined by factors present in an individual from birth 2. Belonging to the essential nature of something
insolvent	adj.	1. Unable to pay debts as they fall due in the usual course of business 2. Relating to or for the relief of insolvents

interference	n.	1. The act or process of interfering; obstruction 2. The disturbing effect of new learning on the performance of previously learned behavior with which it is inconsistent.
judgement	n.	The act or faculty of affirming or denying a conclusion
karma	n.	1. The force generated by a person's actions held in Hinduism and Buddhism to perpetuate transmigration and in its technical ethical consequences to determine his destiny in his next existence 2. Vibration
kanji	n.	A Chinese character; an ideograph
knit	vb.	1. To tie together 2. To link firmly or closely
lascivious	adj.	Lewd; lustful
library	n.	1. Learning resource center 2. A collection resembling or suggesting a library
loom	vb.	To appear in an impressively great or exaggerated appearance of something seen on the horizon or through fog or darkness
marvel	vb.	1. To become filled with surprise, wonder or amazed curiosity 2. TO feel astonishment or perplexity at or about
meishi	n.	Japanese business card
mist	n.	1. Water in the form of particles floating or falling in the atmosphere at or near the surface of the earth and approaching in the form of rain 2. Something that dims or obscures

monolingual	adj.	Knowing or using only one language
multi-racial	adj.	Having several races
myth	n.	1. An usu. Traditional story of ostensibly historical events that serves to unfold part of the world view of a people or explain a practice, belief or natural phenomenon 2. A person or thing having only an imaginary or unverifiable existence
negligence	n.	1. The quality or state of being negligent 2. Failure to exercise the care that a prudent person usu. Exercises
notion	n.	1. An individual's conception or impression of something known, experienced or imagined 2. An inclusive general concept 3. A theory or belief
nostalgia	n.	1. The state of being homesick 2. A wistful or excessively sentimental sometimes abnormal yearning for return to or of some past period or irrecoverable condition
obatarian	n.	Selfish middle-aged women
obsequious	adj.	1. Marked by or exhibiting a fawning attentiveness 2. Subservient
offspring	n.	1. The progency of an animal or plant 2. Product; result
oppressive	adj.	1. The unreasonably burdensome or severe 2. Tyrannical
otakkie	n.	A word derived from "otaku" (home)
pank	n.	Boston accent for park
pawk	n.	New York accent for park
pedagogy	n.	The art, science or profession of teaching
penchant	n.	A strong and continued inclination

periodical	adj.	1. Published with a fixed interval between the issues or numbers 2. Published in, characteristic of, or connected with a periodical
pertinent	adj.	Having a clear decisive relevance to the matter in hand
phoney	adj.	1. Not genuine or real 2. Arousing suspicion
Physical Education	n.	Instruction in the development and care of the body ranging from simple calisthenic exercises to a course of study providing training in hygiene, gymnastics and the performance and management of atheletic games
pitfall	n.	1. Trap; snare 2. A hidden or not easily recognized danger or difficulty
pivot	n.	1. A shaft or pin on which something turns 2. A person, thing or factor having a major or central role, function or effect.
	adj.	Turning on or as if on a pivot
	vb.	To provide with, mount on, or attach by a pivot
plough	n.	1. An implement used to cut, lift and turn over soil esp. in prepairing a seedbed.
pneumonia	n.	A disease of the lungs characterized by inflammation and consolidation followed by resolution and caused by infection or irritants.
pouch	vb.	1. To trespass on 2. To take by illegal methods
post-natal	adj.	Subsequent to birth

premium	n.	1. A reward or recompense for a particular act 2. The consideration paid for a contract of insurance
	adj.	Of exceptional quality or amount
pre-natal	adj.	Occurring, existing or taking place before birth
protagonist	n.	1. The principal character in a story 2. The leader of a cause 3. A muscle that by its contraction actually causes a particular movement
psycholinguistics	n.	The study of linguistic behavior as conditioning and conditioned by psychological factors.
racist	n.	A believer on a belief that race is the primary determinant of human traits and capacities and that racial differences produce an inherent superiority of a particular race.
ramification	n.	1. The act or process of branching. 2. Consequence; outgrowth
receptive	adj.	1. Able or inclined to receive 2. Of a sensory and organ: fit to receive and transmit stimuli
recession	n.	1. The act or action of receding 2. A period of reduced economic activity
redundant	adj.	1. Exceeding what is necessary or normal 2. Characterized by similarity or repetition 3. Profuse; lavish
refugee	n.	One who flees to a foreign country or power to escape danger or persecution
refute	vb.	1. To prove wrong by argument or evidence 2. To deny the truth or accuracy of

repatriate	vb.	To restore or return to the country of origin, allegiance or citizenship
repel	vb.	1. To drive back 2. Turn away; reject
repercussion	n.	1. Reflection; reverberation 2. An action or effect given or exerted in return
repertoire	n.	A list of songs, plays, operas, or the like, that a person or company is prepared to perform.
restraint	n.	1. An act of restraining 2. A control over the expression of one's emotions or thoughts
retaliate	vb.	1. To repay in kind 2. To return like for like; esp.: to get revenge
revamp	vb.	1. To renovate; reconstruct 2. To make over
reverence	n.	1. Honor or respect felt or shown 2. A gesture of respect
revisionist	n.	Advocate of revision
rhapsodize	vb.	To speak or write in a rhapsodic manner
ridiculous	adj.	Laughable; absurd; preposterous
seclusion	n.	1. The act of secluding 2. A secluded or isolated place
skepticism	n.	1. An attitude of doubt or a disposition to incredulity either in general or toward a particular object 2. The doctrine that true knowledge or knowledge in a particular area is uncertain
slogan	n.	1. A war cry or rallying cry 2. A word or phrase used to express a characteristic position or stand or a goal to be achieved

slowdown	n.	A slowing down
slump	vb.	1. To fall or sink suddenly 2. To assume a dropping posture or carriage
	n.	1. A marked or sustained decline esp. in economic activity or prices 2. A downward slide of a mass of rock or land
solidarity	n.	Unity that produce or is based on community of interests, objectives and standards
sovereignty	n.	1. Supreme excellence or an example of it 2. Supreme power esp. over a body politic
specimen	n.	1. An item or part typical of a group or whole 2. Person; individual
spice	n.	1. Any of the various aromatic vegetable products used to season or flavor foods 2. A pungent or fragrant odor
squalor	n.	The quality or state of being squalid.
stereotype	vb.	1. To make a stereotype from 2. To repeat without variation
	n.	1. A plate cast from a printing surface 2. Something conforming to a fixed or general pattern
stilted	adj.	1. Pompous; lofty 2. Having the curved beginning at some distance above the impost
stimulus	adj.	Something that rouses or incites to activity
stripper	n.	1. One that strips 2. A machine that separates a desired part of an agricultural crop

stuff	vb.	1. To fill by packing things in 2. To fill by intellectual effort
subtle	adj.	1. Delicate; elusive 2. Difficult to understand or distinguish
subtlety	n.	The quality or state of being subtle
supplementary	adj.	Added or serving as a supplement
surrealistic	adj.	1. Of or relating to surrealism 2. Having a strange dreamlike atmosphere or quality like that of a surrealist painting
Su-shi	n.	Cold rice dressed with vinegar, shaped into small cakes, and top or wrapped with garnishes
susume	adj.	Japanese world for "advance"
synthetic	n.	Something resulting from synthesis rather occurring naturally
	adj.	Relating to or involving synthesis; not analytic
tedious	adj.	Tiresome because of length of dullness: boring
therapeutic	adj.	1. Of or relating to the treatment of disease or disorders by remedial agents or methods 2. Curative; medicinal
throe	n.	1. Pang; spasm 2. A hard or painful struggle
tilth	n.	1. Cultivated land 2. The state of aggregation of a soil esp. in relation to its suitability for crop growth
toady	vb.	To behave as a toady: engage in sycophancy
toothpick	n.	1. A pointed instrument used for removing food particles lodged between the teeth 2. Wood interdental stimulator

treacherous	adj.	1. Characterized by or manifesting treachery 2. Likely to betray trust: unreliable
triviality	n.	1. The quality or state of being trivial 2. Something trivial
turmoil	n.	A state or condition of extreme confusion, agitation or commotion
tyrannical	adj.	1. Characteristic of a tyrant or tyranny 2. Characterized by oppressive, unjust, or arbitrary behavior or control
unequivocally	adv.	In an unequivocal manner
utopia	n.	1. An imaginary and indefinitely remote place 2. An impractical scheme for social improvement
utterance	n.	1. The last extremity: bitter end 2. Something uttered 3. Vocal expression 4. Power, style or manner of speaking
vague	adj.	1. Not clearly expressed 2. Not clearly defined, grasp or understood
verge	vb.	1. To be contagious 2. To be on the verge or border 3. To be in transition or charge
vernacular	adj.	Using a language or dialect native to a region or country rather than a literary, cultured or foreign language
	n.	1. A vernacular language, expression, or mode of expression 2. The mode of expression of a group or class

vicarious	adj.	1. Serving instead of someone or something else 2. Performed or suffered by one person as a substitute for another or to to the benefit or advantage of another
wife	n.	1. A woman acting in a specified capacity 2. The inside person 3. The old woman 4. The one on the bed 5. The children's mother 6. The cook - according to Chinese

REFERENCES

The Pilipino Journal
International English Newspaper
Dedicated to a stronger Japan-Philippines Brotherhood
203 Takara Toshin Heights
2-14-7 Higashi-Sakura, Higashi-ku, Nayoya 460, Japan

The Filipino News
The Voice of Filipinos in Japan
Published Monthly by Bayanihan Press
IF Koutoku Building
4-12-15 Sakae Naka-ku,
Nagoya Aichi 460, Japan

DK EYEWITNESS TRAVEL GUIDES JAPAN
Published in the United States by DK Publishing Inc.,
375 Hudson Street, New York, New York 10014
Copyright © 2000, 2003 Dorling Kindersley Limited, London
ISSN, 542-1554
ISBN, 0-7894-9719-0

Asahi Shimbun
(Literally Morning Sun Newspaper, English Asahi News)
One of the five national newspaper in Japan.
Nagoya Head Office 3-3, Sakae Itchome,
Naka-ku, Nagoya City, Japan

The Yomiuri Shimbun
1-7-1 Otemachi, Chiyoda-ku, Tokyo 100-8055 Japan
The Japan News is published by the Yomiuri Shimbun, which boasts the largest circulation in the world as the Daily Yomiuri until it was renamed in April 2013. The Japan News draws on the Yomiuri's global news - gathering network to present the latest developments in a wide variety of domestic and international arenas, including politics, economy, sports and culture.

The Mainichi - Japan's National Daily Newspaper since 1922
Tokyo Journal - is an English-language Quarterly magazine about Tokyo and Japan which was established in 1981. The international edition of the magazine was published under the title Japan Journal for a time.

The Japan Times
The Japan Times - Japan - longest 3rd oldest English-language daily newspaper. It is published by a subsidiary of Nifco, is leading manufacturer of plastic fasteners for the automotive and home design industries since 1983
It is headquartered in the Japan Times Nifco Building, Japan Taimuzu "Nifco Biru" in Shibaura, Minato, Tokyo, Japan

www.ingramcontent.com/pod-product-compliance
Lightning Source LLC
Chambersburg PA
CBHW030758180526
45163CB00003B/1076